Top 25 locator map
(continues on inside
back cover)
◄

TwinPack
Madeira

CHRISTOPHER CATLING

Christopher Catling has written more than 30 travel guides. He is a regular contributor to travel magazines on the Internet and in print. His books on London, Florence, Venice and Amsterdam are inspired by a keen interest in art and architecture, while his love of the countryside is reflected in guides to Madeira, Umbria and Crete.

If you have any comments or suggestions for this guide you can contact the editor at *Twinpacks@theAA.com*

AA Publishing
Find out more about AA Publishing and the wide range of services the AA provides by visiting our website at *www.theAA.com*

Contents

About this book

TwinPack Madeira is divided into six sections to cover the six most important aspects of your visit to Madeira. It includes:

- The author's view of the island and its people
- Suggested walks and drives
- The Top 25 Sights to visit
- Features about different aspects of the island that make it special
- Detailed listings of restaurants, hotels, shops and nightlife
- Practical information

In addition, easy-to-read side panels provide fascinating extra facts and snippets, highlights of places to visit and invaluable practical advice.

CROSS-REFERENCES
To help you make the most of your visit, cross-references, indicated by ➤, show you where to find additional information about a place or subject.

MAPS
The Top 25 locator maps found on the inside front and back covers of the book itself are for quick reference. They show the Top 25 Sights, described on pages 24–48, which are clearly plotted by number (**1** – **25**, not page number) in alphabetical order. The grid references given in this book refer to these maps.
The fold-out map in the wallet at the back of the book is a large-scale map of Madeira.

PRICES
Where appropriate, an indication of the cost of an establishment is given by £ signs: £££ denotes higher prices, ££ denotes average prices, while £ denotes lower charges.

MADEIRA
life

A Personal View

MADEIRAN CUISINE

Madeiran cooking is deliciously simple: fish and meat grilled over a charcoal fire and flavoured with garlic and herbs. Eaten with warm bread, straight from the oven, this food is to be savoured in the flower-scented air of a balmy Madeiran evening.

The Madeiran speciality espetada *(beef kebab)*

The traditional bolo de mel *(honey) cake.*

It may be that I fell in love with Madeira because I had just spent three years living in Hong Kong and was sorry to leave behind the climate and scenery of the Far East. Visiting Madeira I discovered a capital city fragrant with the tropical blooms of frangipane and flame-of-the-forest; valleys carved into steps as magnificent as the rice terraces of the Cordilleras in the northern Philippines; and wild woodlands (now declared a World Heritage Site) as dense and as ecologically rich as the rainforests of Sarawak.

So here on Europe's doorstep I discovered an island combining many of the features I had so enjoyed in Southeast Asia, and one that could be reached without the tedium of a long-haul flight. I was hooked, and have since been back many times. Some people think I'm crazy. 'What is there to see and do on such a small island that makes it worth going back so often?' they ask.

Madeira may be small, but it is a place of enormous scenic variety. There are bare volcanic mountain tops with cinder-strewn peaks like the surface of Mars. Red, purple and chocolate-coloured rocks lie scattered around like Liquorice Allsorts. Sunrise and sunset light up the peaks with a swift-changing show of pink, then red, then gold, and the night sky – viewed from this island lost in the middle of the Atlantic – is equally spectacular.

Lush green valleys radiate from the bare mountains down to the sea, clothed in aromatic evergreen trees. Clouds drift up the valleys, dripping moisture to feed the island's lichens and mosses that thrive in the humid atmosphere. Rainstorms, which rarely last long, feed the scores of waterfalls that spill over the cliffs that mark the edges of Madeira. For this is not an island fringed by golden beaches and palm trees – rather it has exactly the type of vertiginous scenery that inspired Turner's paintings or the Romantic poetry of Wordsworth and Coleridge.

Locals play cards in Funchal's Zona Velha

Human hands have added to the island's appeal. Every inch of cultivatable space has been turned into a plot for growing grapes, bananas, sugar cane, exotic fruits and humble cabbages. Steep terraces fill the valley sides, and tiny fields like squares in a patchwork quilt fill the valley bottoms. They are watered by those famous *levadas* – ingenious irrigation canals that follow the island's contours for miles, bringing water from the wet north to the sunny south, and providing walkers with access to some of the island's most remote and beautiful viewpoints.

I have yet to tire of Madeira – I doubt I ever will. My ambition is to stay for a whole year and see the seasons round, enjoying the marvellous show of blooms that never ceases, even in the depths of winter, and enjoying the festivals that seem to take place every weekend. I hope this book will inspire you to discover and enjoy the island as much as I have done – for Madeira truly is a special and unique place.

EVERGREEN

Madeira's native forest is called *laurisilva*, in Portuguese meaning 'laurel-wood' because most of the predominant species belong to the evergreen laurel family. They include the sweetly scented bay tree, used in Madeiran cooking, and the *vinhático*, known as Madeira mahogany and used to make fine furniture.

7

Madeira in Facts and Figures

GEOGRAPHY

- Set in the eastern Atlantic, the island of Madeira lies 1,000km from Lisbon and 600km from Morocco, the nearest mainland.
- Madeira measures 54km by 23km (741sq km) and has a population of 300,000.
- Madeira's nearest neighbour is the island of Porto Santo (population 5,000), which lies 37km to the northeast. Measuring just 106sq km, the island is blessed with a magnificent 11km sweep of sandy beach.
- Also part of the Madeiran archipelago are two groups of uninhabited islands: the three Ilhas Desertas (Desert Isles), situated 16km to the southeast of Madeira, and the Ilhas Selvagens (Savage Isles), which lie 216km to the south.

LANDSCAPE

- Madeira is the product of volcanic eruptions that took place 20 million years ago. Volcanic peaks are a major feature of the island, several of them rising to more than 1,800m.
- Christopher Columbus described Madeira to Queen Isabella of Spain by crumpling up a piece of paper: apart from the southern coastal plain, the mountainous island is carved into myriad deep valleys and ravines.
- Driving distances are greatly magnified by the steep terrain, necessitating slow progress along the tortuous zig-zagging roads.

CLIMATE

- Madeira's climate is sub-tropical: the southerly latitude ensures warm, frost-free winters and cooling Atlantic winds take the edge off the intense heat of summer.
- Atlantic fronts drop rain on the north side of the island, while the south side remains dry and sunny for much of the year.
- Temperatures average around 24°C during the summer, dropping to around 19°C in winter.

ECONOMY

- Madeira's fortune was built on sugar production in the 15th to 17th centuries.
- The production of Madeira wine sustained the island in the 18th and 19th centuries.
- Today, tourism is the biggest revenue earner.

People of Madeira

Christopher Columbus (1451–1506)

Working as a buyer for a group of Lisbon-based sugar merchants, Christopher Columbus made three visits to Madeira. On his first visit, in 1478, he sought out the company of his compatriot Bartolomeu Perestrelo, governor of the island of Porto Santo. Not long after, he married Perestrelo's daughter, Dona Filipa Moniz. Their child, Diego, was born in 1479, but Dona Filipa died in 1480. During his stay, Columbus became convinced by the vegetation washed up on Porto Santo's shores that there must be land beyond the western horizon. Twelve years later he persuaded the Castilian monarchs, Ferdinand and Isabella, to fund the voyage that proved his hunch to be correct.

Napoleon Bonaparte (1769–1821)

The emperor Napoleon was an involuntary visitor to Madeira in 1815, when the ship carrying him to exile on St Helena moored in Funchal harbour. The British Consul, Henry Veitch, went on board and gave the vanquished emperor gifts of fruit and books. Veitch was subsequently dismissed from his post for addressing Napoleon as 'Your Majesty', though Lord Palmerston later reinstated him. Napoleon is said to have ordered a barrel of Madeira wine, which he paid for with some gold coins that were later placed ceremoniously under the foundation stone of the island's neoclassical English Church, completed in 1822.

Winston Churchill (1874–1965)

Napoleon never drank his barrel of Madeira. Instead it was returned to the island in 1822, where it continued to mature. More than a century later, in 1950, Winston Churchill chose to spend a holiday here, painting the coastal scenery around Câmara de Lobos and enjoying the hospitality at the elegant Reid's Hotel. At a dinner given in his honour, he was presented with a bottle of 'the Napoleon Madeira'. Sharing this with his fellow guests, he reminded them that 'when this wine was made, Marie Antoinette was still alive'.

A bronze statue of Christopher Columbus, at the Santa Catarina Gardens

LAST RESTING PLACE

Buried in a plain black coffin in Monte church is the Emperor Charles I (1887–1922), last of the Austro-Hungarian Habsburg emperors. Charles succeeded at the death of his great uncle, Franz Joseph, in 1916, but was deposed at the end of World War I. After deportation to Switzerland he chose to spend the rest of his brief life in exile on Madeira.

A Chronology

20 million BC	Madeira is formed through volcanic eruptions.
1.7 million BC	The Madeiran volcanoes become extinct, the lava cools and storms erode the weaker rocks to create deep valleys and ravines.
AD 77	Pliny mentions the Madeiran archipelago in his Natural History, calling them the 'Purple Islands' after the reddish-purple dye obtained from the sap of the island's dragon trees.
1351	The Medici Map, now in the Laurentian Library in Florence, depicts three islands off the African coast named Porto Santo, Deserta and Isola de Lolegname (Italian for Wooded Isle).
1370s	English merchant Robert Machin and his lover, Anne of Hereford, are shipwrecked on Madeira. Madeira's second-largest town, Machico, was later founded on the spot where Anne died and, it is said, named in the couple's honour.
1418	João Gonçalves Zarco is blown out to sea by a storm while exploring the west coast of Africa. Having found a safe anchorage off Porto Santo, he returns to Lisbon to report his sighting of a mist- and wood-covered island on the horizon.
1419	Prince Henry the Navigator sends a fleet, headed by Zarco, to explore the islands further.
1420	Zarco lands on Madeira (Wooded) and claims it for Portugal. The island is set alight as the fastest way of clearing land for settlement.
1425	Madeira is officially declared a province of Portugal. Zarco, governor of the western half of the island, founds Funchal; Tristão Vaz, governor of the east, founds Machico; and Bartolomeu Perestrelo colonises Porto Santo.
1452	Madeira's sub-tropical climate and fertile volcanic soils prove ideal for sugar cultivation.
1478	Christopher Columbus visits Madeira, which has now become a major sugar producer.

1514	According to the first official census, Madeira now has 5,000 inhabitants (excluding slaves) and Funchal is Portugal's third most populous city, after Lisbon and Porto.
1566	Some 1,000 French pirates raid Funchal, the capital, killing the governor and 250 Madeirans.
1580	Madeira comes under Spanish rule after Philip II conquers Portugal.
1640	The Portuguese revolt against Spanish rule and regain independence under King João IV.
1662	By marrying Catherine of Braganza, Charles II gains trading concessions for English merchants, which paves the way for their eventual domination of the Madeira wine trade.
1852	After mildew devastates the island's vineyards, new, more resilient vine varieties are planted.
1891	Reid's Hotel opens its doors, catering for the increasing number of wealthy visitors over-wintering in Madeira.
1964	Madeira's isolation ends with the opening of Santa Catarina airport.
1974	Portugal becomes a democracy after soldiers overthrow the post-war dictatorship, with flowers in their gun-barrels to symbolise their peaceful intentions.
1976	Madeira becomes an autonomous region, with its own parliament.
1986	Portugal's European Union membership releases development funds for improving Madeira's infrastructure, bringing electricity and roads to remote rural communities.
1997	The opening of the island's new south-coast expressway transforms transport on the island.
2002	Euro notes and coins are introduced in Madeira.

Best of Madeira

If you only have a short time on Madeira, or would like to gain a rounded picture of the island, be sure to experience the following highlights:

A bottle of vintage Madeira

- Spend a day in Funchal (➤ 30–37), with its mosaic-patterned streets, its embroidery shops and its elegant town houses.
- Step back in time on a visit to the Adegas de São Francisco wine lodge (➤ 31) to learn about the history of Madeira wine production.
- Go for dinner in Funchal's Zona Velha (Old Town, ➤ 30) and listen to the plaintive and haunting sound of Portuguese *fado* music.
- Ride on the Teleféricos da Madeira (Madeira Cable Car, ➤ 48) and enjoy stunning views on the way up to Monte. Then brace yourself for the Monte Toboggan Ride on the way down (➤ 40).
- Spend a night in the hotel on top of Pico do Arieiro (➤ 41), Madeira's third-highest peak, to enjoy the scintillating colours of the Madeiran sunset, or to wonder at the mass of stars in the crystal-clear night sky.
- Visit the Quinta do Palheiro Ferreiro (➤ 44), also known as Blandy's Garden, to see the flowers and shrubs of several continents artfully blended to create a fascinating garden.
- Take a walk along a *levada* (irrigation canal, ➤ 20–21), penetrating deep into the peaceful heart of the Madeiran countryside.
- Drive from São Vicente to Porto Moniz along the scenically spectacular northern coast of Madeira, through rock-cut tunnels and beneath waterfalls (➤ 54).
- Join in a village festival (➤ 22) for the fun of noisy fireworks and to taste *espetada* (beef kebabs) cooked over an open wood fire.
- Take a trip to Curral das Freiras (➤ 29) to marvel at the scenic beauty of this hidden valley at the island's heart.
- Visit the Whaling Museum (➤ 28) at Caniçal to learn about plans to provide protection for these captivating sea mammals, and loiter on the nearby beach to watch the fishermen land their catch or work on their boats.

Rua do Carmo, in Funchal's Zona Velha (Old Town)

MADEIRA
how to organise your time

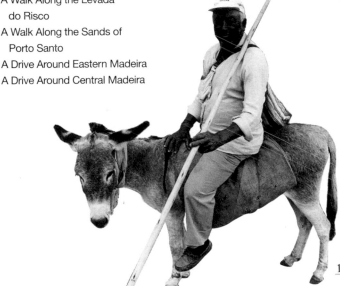

A Walk Exploring Funchal's Architecture

INFORMATION

Distance 1km
Time 30 minutes
Start point Câmara Municipal
(Town Hall), Praça do
Município
✚ b2
End point British Cemetery,
Rua da Carreira. (To enter,
ring the bell at No. 235)
✚ a2
Lunch O Pátio Café
✉ Rua da Carreira 43
☎ 227 376

Discover Funchal's rich architectural heritage on a stroll through the city centre.

Start at the Câmara Municipal (Town Hall). The elegant 18th-century mansion was built for the wealthy Count of Carvalhal but was sold by his profligate heirs. The delightful palm-filled courtyard features a graceful sculpture of Leda and the Swan (1880). Turn your back on the entrance to view Praça do Município (Town Square), paved with grey basalt and white marble in a fish-scale pattern. To the right, gesticulating saints decorate the façade of the Igreja di Colégio, the Jesuit church, founded in 1574. To the left is the Bishop's Palace of 1600, now home to the Museu de Arte Sacra (Sacred Art Museum, ➤ 34).

Cross the square, heading for the far right-hand corner. Walk up shop-lined Rua C Pestana and carry straight on at the next junction, along Rua da Carreira.

Three doors up on the left, in Rua da Carreira, is the entrance to the Pátio complex, with its bookshops and courtyard café. Try coffee here, or buy typical Madeiran *bolo de mel* (literally 'honey cake' but actually made with molasses) at the baker's further up on the left.

Walk up Rua da Carreira. As you dip in and out of the street's characterful shops, look up to see the pretty wrought-iron balconies that decorate many of the upper storeys. Among the best houses is No. 155.

The third turn right (Rua do Quebra Costas) leads to the English Church (completed 1822), set in a pretty garden. At the end of Rua da Carreira is the British Cemetery (Cimitero Inglesa), the burial ground of Madeira's Protestants of all nationalities, worth visiting for its many poignant 19th-century memorials and epitaphs.

Top: *the Câmara Municipal (Town Hall)*
Above: *intricate wrought-iron balconies look out onto Rua da Carreira*

A Walk Around Funchal Harbour

Early evening is a good time to do this walk, ending up with a view from a pavement café of Madeira's brief sunset.

Start at the tourist office in Avenida Arriaga and turn right. Funchal's residents gather to chat in the tree-shaded Jardim de São Francisco, to the right of the Adegas de São Francisco wine lodge (➤ 31). Opposite is the remarkable 1920s Toyota showroom, decorated with tile pictures of the Monte Toboggan Ride (➤ 40). Next door is the Municipal Theatre of 1888 (you can go and look inside if there is no performance) and the trendy theatre bar, with its own tree-shaded patio, alongside.

Turn left beside the theatre, down Rua do Conselheiro José Silvestre Ribeiro. At the bottom, on the left, is the Casa do Turista (➤ 76), an elegantly furnished town house packed with quality products from Madeira and mainland Portugal.

Turn right, if you wish, to walk through the busy port and out along the Molhe da Pontinha, the great sea wall that encloses the harbour. Alternatively, cross to the sea wall side of Avenida do Mar and turn left.

The 16th-century Palaçio de São Lourenço (➤ 53) on your left bristles with ancient cannon. To your right is the yacht marina, enclosed by a high sea wall painted by visiting sailors with pictures recording their visit. Seafood restaurants line the landward side, while ice-cream booths and floating restaurants lie further up along Avenida do Mar. Beyond, on the left, is the Madeiran Regional Parliament, with its circular modern debating chamber.

Turn left up the street just before this building to reach the cathedral square (➤ 37), with its many pavement cafés.

INFORMATION

Distance 1.5km
Time 1 hour
Start point Tourist Information Centre, Avenida Arriaga 16
➕ b2
End point Largo da Sé
➕ b2
Lunch Marina Terrace (££)
✉ Marina do Funchal
☎ 230 547

A fishing boat enters Funchal harbour in the soft evening light

15

A Walk Along the Levada do Risco

INFORMATION

Distance 3km
Time 1 hour
Start/end point Rabaçal
government rest house
🚏 B2
Lunch No cafés in the area;
take a picnic and water

If you are driving across the Paúl da Serra, it is worth breaking your journey to explore this secret valley of ancient trees and waterfalls.

Rabaçal is reached down a precipitous, single-track road off the Paúl da Serra plateau. (There are very few passing places on the road so if you are feeling energetic you may prefer to park at the top and walk down). Once in Rabaçal, there is a car park alongside the government rest house (used by forestry workers, but with picnic tables, barbecue pits and toilets for walkers).

Follow the sign to the right of the car park which points down the track to the Levada do Risco. The Levada do Risco watercourse is cut into a hillside cloaked in huge, gnarled tree heathers. The humid air has also encouraged the growth of magnificent lichens, some resembling apple-coloured seaweed, some more like hanks of grey-green hair. Local foresters use branches from the tree heather for fencing along the route.

*The Levada do Risco
runs alongside a steep
rock face*

After five minutes' walking, a path leads off to the left, signposted Levada das 25 Fontes (the Levada of the 25 Springs). Ignore this for now and carry straight on.

After another ten minutes you will come to the Risco waterfall, pouring down from the rocky heights into a magical fern-hung bowl. To your left there are sweeping views down into the green valley of the River Janela.

Return the way you came. You can extend your walk by taking the more difficult Levada das 25 Fontes, following the signposted path downhill and then turning right once you reach the *levada*. This will take you, after a 20-minute walk, to another fine waterfall with one main cascade and many smaller ones.

A Walk Along the Sands of Porto Santo

You can take a couple of hours to walk the 6.5km from Vila Baleira (▶ 43) to Ponta da Calheta, or you can spend all day, stopping to swim, sunbathe or laze around in beach cafés.

▶ 43

Follow Avenue Dr M Pestana Junior, the coastal road, westwards out of Vila Baleira. Shortly after passing the church of Espirito Santo, at Campo de Baixo, turn right up a road signposted to Pedreira (Quarry).

INFORMATION

Distance 6.5km
Time 2 hours 30 minutes
Start point Vila Baleira
End point Ponta da Calheta
Lunch Pôr-do-Sol (£££)
✉ Ponta da Calheta
☎ 984 380

Occasionally you will pass ruined farm buildings and the stumps and stone towers of ancient windmills surviving from the time when wheat was grown on Porto Santo. The quarry, when you reach it, has exposed rock patterned like organ pipes.

The road – really a potholed track – continues round the low hill called Pico de Ana Ferreira (283m), and rejoins the coast road at Ponta. Turn right at Ponta and continue until the road runs out at Ponta da Calheta (▶ 60).

▶ 60

The café here is a good spot to enjoy a long lazy lunch and views that, on a clear day, stretch to Madeira.

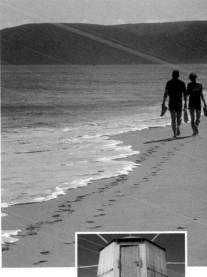

Afterwards, you can take bus No. 4 back to Vila Baleira (last departure 6:20PM) or enquire at the Pôr-do-Sol about their free shuttle bus service. Alternatively, if you still have the energy, you can follow the sands back to Vila Baleira.

The beach remains idyllically unspoiled, with room for all comers, from windsurfers and sun worshippers to the Madeirans who bury themselves in the sands, believing them to have therapeutic properties.

Top: *the golden sands of Porto Santo's beach*
Above: *the owner of a windmill at Camacha*

17

A Drive Around Eastern Madeira

INFORMATION

Distance 60km
Time 6 hours
Start/end point Funchal
🔀 D4
Lunch O Relógio (££)
✉ Largo da Achada,
Camacha
☎ 922 114
🕐 12–4, 7–11

Allow at least half a day for this leisurely drive around Madeira's eastern spur, including time to swim off one of the island's few naturally sandy beaches.

Leave Funchal on the EN 101, following signs to the airport, then turn left, after 3km, onto the EN 102, signposted to Camacha.

After 2km turn right to visit the Blandy wine-merchant family's splendid Quinta do Palheiro Ferreiro gardens (➤ 44).

Rejoin the EN 102 and continue north to Camacha (➤ 26). Continue along the EN 102 for a further 11km to Santo António da Serra.

At Santo António da Serra take a stroll in the park surrounding the Quinta da Serra, the home of the Blandy family before they acquired the Quinta do Palheiro Ferreiro.

Continue along the EN 101 but turn left, before reaching Machico, on the EN 101-3 sign-posted to Caniçal. Skirt Caniçal and continue to the end of the road for a walk out across the cliff tops at Ponta do São Lourenço (➤ 54).

Viewed from across the bay, the concrete pillars which support the runway of Madeira's airport

Cool off by taking a dip in the sea at Prainha beach (➤ 58) on the way back to Caniçal, with its Whaling Museum (➤ 28). Stop at Machico (➤ 38), Madeira's second town, to walk around the bay and visit the three historic churches.

Follow the coastal road beneath the airport runway to Santa Cruz (➤ 51).

Depending on the time of day, your last stop before returning to Funchal could be Garajau (➤ 50), where you can watch the sun go down from the cliff top alongside the outsize statue of Christ.

A Drive Around Central Madeira

This drive takes a whole day, encompassing fishing ports and wave-battered cliffs, green valleys and volcanic peaks.

Start early and head for Câmara de Lobos (➤ 27), hoping to catch the last of the bustle surrounding the town's fish market. Continue to Cabo Girão (➤ 25) for the dizzying views from Europe's second-highest sea cliff.

At Ribeira Brava (➤ 45) you can enjoy a reviving cup of coffee in a seafront café before exploring the Manueline Church of São Bento.

Drive north up the terraced slopes of the valley of the Ribeira Brava to Boca da Encumeada (➤ 24) for views of the northern and southern coast of Madeira. Descend through woodland to São Vicente (➤ 51) and then follow the meandering north coast eastwards.

You may want to stop and swim at Ponta Delgada (➤ 58) before continuing on to Santana (➤ 47) for lunch, shopping or to explore the triangular houses.

If you are feeling energetic, consider climbing Pico Ruivo, although clouds may hinder the views in the afternoon (➤ 42). Alternatively, continue to Faial (➤ 54) and drive south to Ribeiro Frio (➤ 46) for a gentle stroll to Balcões. A third option is to continue on to the Poiso pass and drive west to the summit of Pico do Arieiro (➤ 41). From the Poiso pass the road descends via Terreiro da Luta (➤ 55) to Monte (➤ 39), where you can visit the Monte Palace Tropical Garden before the short drive back to Funchal.

INFORMATION

Distance 120km
Time 8 hours
Start/end point Funchal
✚ D4
Lunch O Colmo
✉ Santana, main street
☎ 573 666

The village of São Vicente, with its sparkling baroque houses and parish church

19

Finding Peace and Quiet

EXPLORE MADEIRA'S HEART

On Madeira you can escape quickly and easily from the bustle of modern life by walking alongside the island's extensive network of irrigation canals. Called *levadas*, these watercourses link village to village and penetrate deep into the mountainous heart of the island. *Levadas* follow the island's contours, falling with an almost imperceptible gradient so it is possible to walk for miles on level paths, enjoying Madeira's exhilarating landscapes with none of the physical effort normally associated with mountain climbing. Along the route you will encounter shady eucalyptus forest, fragrant with menthol, sun-dappled clearings where butterflies feed, banks of hydrangeas and amaryllis, rural farms and orchards, rock-cut tunnels and waterfalls.

THE WORK OF CENTURIES

Levadas are as old as the earliest settlement on Madeira. The first rock-cut irrigation canals were dug in the 15th century using slave and convict labour. Over the centuries, more and more canals were dug to distribute water from

the upland areas, where rainfall is plentiful, to the banana plantations, vineyards and terraced fields of the sunny south side of Madeira. Today, the canal network extends to more than 2,150km; it is fed by naturally occurring springs and

Basking lizards may well be seen adorning a wall or rock

purpose-built reservoirs. As well as irrigating the fields, the *levadas* supply water to several of the island's electricity-generating power stations.

Maintaining the *levadas* is the task of the *levadeiro*, who patrols a stretch of watercourse, clearing landslips and fallen debris. He also operates the sluices that channel the water to different farms along the route according to a pre-arranged timetable.

LEVADA WALKING

Most *levadas* are easy to find and follow, but proper precautions should still be taken. Some *levadas* pass through long tunnels, so you need to take a torch with plenty of battery power. Many paths cross aqueducts or cling to steep hillsides with a sheer drop to one or both sides: anyone who suffers from vertigo should beware. Comfortable walking shoes will prevent blisters, and they need to be slip-proof to avoid accidents on wet and mossy paths. Be prepared for all types of weather, ranging from a sudden shower to blistering sun.

If you want to sample a *levada*, try one of the short and easy-to-follow walks detailed in this book (see the Rabaçal route, ➤ 16, or the Balcões walk, ➤ 46). Alternatively, you can join a guided tour led by a knowledgeable local guide (further details from the tourist office in Funchal or through travel agencies on the island).

Once you have found your feet you can set off on your own, perhaps guided by John and Pat Underwood's *Landscapes of Madeira* (published by Sunflower Books; copies can be bought at the Funchal tourist office and in most bookshops on Madeira). The book details more than 80 walks of different length and character: whichever you choose, you can be sure that the gentle sound of running water will accompany your every step, and that exhilarating views are guaranteed.

A poker-straight section of the Levada da Roda

A levada winds through the woodlands

What's On

JANUARY

Grand New Year Firework Show (midnight on 31 Dec): the New Year starts with a bang and noisy blowing of ships' hooters at one of Europe's most spectacular public fireworks festivals.

Dia de Reis (6 Jan): the Day of the Kings, with its religious services, marks the end of the Christmas and New Year celebrations.

FEBRUARY

Carnival (four days before Ash Wednesday): Carnival is celebrated all over Madeira, but the parades in Funchal are definitely the best. On the Saturday before Ash Wednesday bands accompany a costumed parade, with clowns, dancers and people in spectacular fancy dress. Three days later the so-called Local Parade includes satirical floats that poke fun at local politicians.

APRIL

Flower Festival (second or third weekend): Funchal becomes a blaze of colour for this festival as shops, houses and churches are all decorated with ribbons and flags, and children make a wall of flowers in Praça do Município. The climax is a parade through Funchal.

JUNE

Fins de Semana Musicais Musical Weekends (all month): guest musicians and talented students from the local conservatoire perform in the cathedral and the Teatro Baltazar Dias.

AUGUST

Feast of the Assumption (15 Aug): Madeira's biggest religious festival is celebrated with religious services by day and dancing, fireworks and feasting by night. Penitents visit the church at Monte to climb the steps on their knees.

SEPTEMBER

Madeira Wine Festival (13–15 Sep): in Funchal and Câmara de Lobos, the completion of the wine harvest is celebrated with wine-treading demonstrations, music, dance and wine tastings.

OCTOBER

Festa da Maçã (25–26 Oct): the Apple Festival in Camacha offers an opportunity to sample the apples grown around Camacha, and to enjoy local folk singing, dancing, cider and apple brandy.

NOVEMBER

Festa da Castanha (1 Nov): celebrates the chestnut harvest in Curral das Freiras.

DECEMBER

Christmas Illuminations (from 8 Dec): the build-up to Christmas begins when the street illuminations are switched on by a local dignitary.

Christmas Cribs (from 16 Dec): the Portuguese tradition of building tableaux representing the crib continues in Funchal, and in many villages.

MADEIRA's
top 25 sights

The sights are shown on the maps on the inside front cover and inside back cover, numbered **1**–**25** alphabetically

Boca da Encumeada

Choose a bright, clear day for your visit to the Boca da Encumeada and the stunning views could stretch as far as the north and south coasts.

The Boca da Encumeada (Encumeada Pass), midway between Ribeira Brava and São Vicente, is a popular stopping-off point for round-the-island tours because of the extensive views to be had from the lookout point at the top of the pass (1,004m). Weather permitting, it is possible to see across to São Vicente on the north coast and down the Serra de Água Valley to the south coast, though more often than not you will stand in brilliant sunshine looking down on to the top of humid rain clouds.

If the weather is finer and clear, prolong your visit by following the Levada do Norte (Levada of the North) westwards: look for the sign to Folhadal opposite the café and climb up to the *levada* past the keeper's house. It is well worth exploring this path for 2km or so; you will be greeted by an abundance of wild flowers and excellent views to the south.

INFORMATION

➕ C2

✉ On EN 104 road, 43km northwest of Funchal

🍴 Café (£) alongside the viewpoint car park; for more substantial meals try Restaurante Encumeada (££, ☎ 952 319), on the road south to Serra de Água

🚌 Bus 139

↔ Ribeira Brava (➤ 45)

The cloud-capped Encumeada Pass and the surrounding mountains

Cabo Girão

The towering cliff face of Cabo Girão can be viewed from below or from the dizzy heights of its cliff-top balcony.

Cabo Girão is not quite Europe's highest sea cliff – it is beaten into second place by a Norwegian competitor – but at 580m it is impressive enough. Girão means 'turning', an apt description of the vertiginous effect of looking down to the sea from the cliff top. In fact, it is said that the name dates from Zarco's first voyage of discovery when he set out to explore the Madeiran coast in 1420. His diary vividly describes sailing 'towards a dark, stupendous object... abode of demons and evil spirits'. Deciding to venture no further, Zarco turned back at this point to seek a safe anchorage at what is now the fishing port of Câmara de Lobos.

For a different view of Cabo Girão you can retrace Zarco's voyage by taking a boat excursion along Madeira's southern coast. Numerous companies offer tours from Funchal, and you can either book direct by visiting the marina, or through hotels and travel agents. Half-day tours go as far west as Ponta do Sol (➤ 50), and most operators anchor off Cabo Girão so you can swim in the clean, warm waters. Turispeca (➤ side panel) also offers fishing trips.

Whether you choose to view Cabo Girão from above or below, look out for the tiny terraces cut into the cliff face, where brave and hardy farmers cultivate vines on pocket-handkerchief-sized plots, taking advantage of the warmth stored in these south-facing rocks.

When you've soaked up the view, visit the small pavilion by the *miradouro* car park, where there is a photographic exhibition from the Museu Photographia Vicentes. On display are photos of famous visitors to Madeira, including Winston Churchill and George Bernard Shaw.

INFORMATION

- ✚ C4
- ✉ 22km west of Funchal, and 10km west of Câmara de Lobos
- 🕐 Pavilion: daily 9–6
- 🍴 Snack bar (£) alongside the viewing platform
- 🚌 Bus 154 from Funchal
- 🚢 Details of boat excursions from the tourist office in Funchal (✉ Avenida Arriaga 16 ☎ 229 057) or through companies based in the yacht marina, such as Turispeca (☎ 231 063) and Costa do Sol (☎ 238 538)
- ♿ Few
- 🔁 Câmara de Lobos (➤ 27)

Camacha

INFORMATION

✚ E3
✉ 16km northeast of Funchal
🚌 Buses 29, 77
♿ Few

O Relógio
✉ Largo da Achada, Camacha
☎ 922 777
🕐 Open daily 9–6, except public hols
🍴 Café (£) on the ground floor of O Relógio

A wicker-worker crafts the seat of a chair

Camacha is *the* place for wicker on Madeira – and when you've finished browsing you can enjoy the fine views.

Camacha sits on a high plateau to the northeast of Funchal. To enjoy the panoramic views to be had from this elevated position, you have to visit the café called O Relógio (The Clock), on the main square. This former *quinta* (rural mansion) sports a squat clock tower, whose clock and bell were brought here from Liverpool in 1896 by the philanthropical Dr Michael Grabham. Grabham was an expert, among other things, on Madeiran flora, tropical fish, organs, clocks, volcanoes and electro-magnetism; once asked how he could speak with such erudition on so many subjects, he replied: 'What I do not know, I make up'.

In addition to the café and restaurant, O Relógio is the largest outlet on the island for Madeira's distinctive wicker products. Baskets and furniture fill every inch of available space – hanging from the ceilings as well as being piled on the floors – and nobody will pressurise you to buy as you explore the packed rooms.

Wicker is produced from the pollarded willows which thrive in the warm and humid valleys around Camacha. Cut back to a stunted and knobbly trunk each winter, the willows put out whip-like shoots, called osiers, up to 3m in length. These are placed in tanks and soaked in water until the bark is sufficiently pliable to be peeled from the core. Bundles of osiers are then delivered to the cottages of wicker-workers, who boil the canes to make them supple before weaving them into everything imaginable, from simple place mats and wastepaper baskets, to peacock-backed chairs or ornate birdcages.

Demonstrations of wicker-weaving can sometimes be seen in the O Relógio basement, while the middle floor has a display of Noah's Ark animals and a galleon made by local weavers.

Câmara de Lobos

This much-photographed coastal village owes its appeal to its small fleet of colourful fishing boats.

The boats of Câmara de Lobos, brightly painted in primary colours, are drawn up on the town's small pebble beach for much of the day. On the eastern side of the harbour there is a small boatyard where you can watch boats being made and repaired. Local fishermen go out at night to catch *espada* (scabbard fish), which live at depths of 800m or more (hence their big eyes, needed to see in the gloom). At night they come up to feed, and that is when they are most easily caught, using long lines, each with 150 or so hooks, baited with squid.

To see the catch being brought in you need to be up early: by 7AM most of the fish will have been cleaned and sent off to Funchal's market. The fishermen, meanwhile, celebrate the night's catch by filling the local bars. Heavy drinking is blamed for the evident poverty that you will encounter in the village, especially in the alleys leading west from the harbour, where large families live in tiny single-roomed houses, crammed up against the cliff face. Here you will also find the simple fishermen's chapel of Nossa Senhora da Conceição, its walls painted with naive scenes showing the Apostles fishing on the shores of Lake Galilee, and the miracles of St Nicholas, patron saint of seafarers. Further west, up the hill, is the larger Church of São Sebastian, with its *azulejos* and statue of the saint.

INFORMATION

➕ C4

✉ 14km west of Funchal

🍴 Good choice of cafés and restaurants (£–££), including Churchill's Place (££, ☎ 944 336), on the east side of the harbour

🚌 Most westbound buses go to Câmara de Lobos, including 4, 6, 107, 154

♿ None

↔ Cabo Girão (➤ 25)

❓ The Feast of St Peter the Fisherman is celebrated with a lively festival in Câmara de Lobos on 29 Jun

Taking a break on a colourful fishing boat

Caniçal

INFORMATION

➕ F3

✉ 32km east of Funchal

🍴 Cafés (£) next to the
   museum and alongside
   the seafront

🚌 Bus 113

♿ Few

🔄 Machico (➤ 38)

Museu de Baleia

✉ Largo da Lota

☎ 961 407

🕐 Tue–Sun 10–12, 1–6.
   Closed Mon

💰 Moderate

Caniçal was the last place in southern Europe to stop whaling. It is now home to a whale-conservation museum and a thriving fishing industry.

Caniçal's days as a major whaling station ended in 1981, when the trade was banned by international treaty. Instrumental in the process of achieving the ban was the Society for the Protection of Marine Mammals, which helped establish the small but informative Museu de Baleia (Whaling Museum), now located in the offices once used by the Caniçal whaling company. Videos and displays in the museum explain how retired Madeiran fishermen have turned from whale hunting to conservation, putting their knowledge of sperm whale habits and migration patterns at the disposal of marine biologists, who hope to establish a marine mammal sanctuary around Madeira.

For a reminder of Caniçal's whaling past, watch John Huston's 1956 film *Moby Dick*, which used shots of the village's whaling fleet.

Nowadays, the brightly coloured boats drawn up on the pebbly shore alongside Caniçal's museum belong to Madeira's biggest tuna fleet; it is fascinating to stand and watch the fishermen maintaining and repairing them, using timeless craft techniques.

Top: *Caniçal's Whaling Museum*
Above: *brightly painted fishing boats in Caniçal harbour*

You may also see the fishermen preparing the long baited lines that are sunk to great depths to catch scabbard fish. Some of their nightly catch is processed in the big refrigeration plant near the dock, then shipped to mainland Portugal.

Curral das Freiras

This secret valley, known as the Nun's Corral (or Refuge), is hidden among the peaks of Madeira's central mountain range.

INFORMATION

+ C3
* 20km northwest of Funchal
* Choice of restaurants (£) in the centre of the village
* Bus 81 from Funchal (you may find the journey hair-raising, with its zig-zag bends and sheer cliff edges)
* None
* Free

Only with mild exaggeration did H N Coleridge, nephew of the poet, describe Curral das Freiras as 'one of the great sights of the world'. The majestic peaks that encircle the village certainly invite such claims, though quiet contemplation of the views can sometimes be difficult because of the sheer number of visitors in high season.

A first glimpse of the hidden valley is to be had from the lookout point high above the village, signposted Eira do Serrado (Eagle's Nest). From here, the village seems to sit in the bowl of a vast crater, surrounded by sheer cliffs rising to jagged peaks. The view is not quite so enthralling from the bottom looking up, but there are other compensations: bars in Curral das Freiras sell the local speciality, a delicious chestnut-flavoured liqueur called *licor de castanha*.

If you enjoy bustle, go to Curral das Freiras on a Sunday, when a lively market spreads through the network of streets around the parish church. If not, the best way to find relative solitude is to walk into the village along the old zig-zag path that starts from the Eira do Serrado car park.

Until 1959, this path was the only way in and out of the village. Its impregnability was the reason why the nuns of Santa Clara Convent (▶ 55) fled here in 1566 to escape from piratical raids on Funchal. The first stage of the path is rough but it soon becomes a cobbled track. It takes around two hours to walk down and there are said to be 52 hairpin bends on the way.

The dizzying view of Curral das Freiras, from the Eira do Serrado viewpoint

29

Funchal

INFORMATION

⊞ D4

🍴 Some of the city's best restaurants are in the Zona Velha (£–££)

🅸 Avenida Arriaga 16

☎ 225 658

Far from being the provincial island backwater you might expect from its remote location, Madeira's capital is a bustling city of 100,000 people. Visitors from mainland Portugal often refer to it as 'Little Lisbon'.

Funchal means 'fennel' and the city's name is said to derive from the abundance of fennel plants that Zarco, the island's discoverer, found growing here when he arrived in 1420. Zarco chose this spot to found the future capital because of its sheltered natural harbour, which is today filled with every kind of vessel, from rusty container ships to luxurious cruise liners.

Funchal's streets twist and tumble up and down the steep hillside that rises from the harbour. Only in the city centre are the streets level, and here the main avenues are paved with black and white mosaic-work patterns.

The city is divided into three sectors by its rivers, now enclosed between high embankments to prevent flash floods.

In the eastern sector is the Zona Velha, or Old Town, with its many restaurants, some offering *fado* music. Formerly the city's slum, it is now an area of quaint cobbled streets with craft shops occupying the low, one-roomed houses where at one time whole families slept, ate and played. There is a tiny black-pebble beach (the Praia da Barreirinha) where local people come to bathe and eat grilled sardines sold by street vendors.

The central sector of the city contains a jumble of embroidery factories, crumbling town houses and shops selling pungent salt cod or dried herbs.

High above the harbour, on the cliff tops west of the city, is the Hotel Zone. The area is almost a self-contained town, with its tourist shops and supermarkets, cinemas and restaurants.

A shopkeeper displays an intricately embroidered tablecloth

Funchal's Adegas de São Francisco

Visit a wine lodge set in a medieval monastery to sample Madeira and learn how it is produced. You'll realise what Churchill meant when he said 'to drink Madeira is to sip history with every glass'.

To step from the bustle of Funchal's main street into the calm courtyards of the Adegas de São Francisco (St Francis Wine Lodge) is to enter a world where time has a different meaning. Here, on payment of a fairly substantial sum, you can buy wines that were bottled in the 1860s, while upstairs, slowly maturing in huge barrels of Brazilian satinwood and American oak, are wines that nobody living today is likely to taste.

The lodge, with its romantic timber buildings and wisteria-hung balconies, started life as the monastery of St Francis and was converted to its present use in 1834. At that time, Madeira wines were still being sent on board ship to the equator and back in the belief that the rocking motion improved the wine. The production process was revolutionised by the accidental discovery that Madeira's unique quality comes not from motion but from gentle heating. Now the wine is 'cooked' in vast vats using the warmth of the sun, boosted when necessary by the heat from hot water pipes. All this becomes clear as you tour the cobbled yard to see ancient wooden presses and leather-bound wine ledgers, learn the subtle arts of the wine blender and visit the warming rooms, with their deliciously heady smell of old wood and wine. Scents such as these are a prelude to the pleasures to come as you head for the sampling that concludes this popular tour, which takes place in a room with delightful murals painted in 1922 by Max Romer.

INFORMATION

- ✚ b2
- ✉ Avenida Arriaga 28, Funchal
- ☎ 740 110
- 🕐 Guided tours: Mon–Fri 10:30, 3:30; Sat 11. Closed Sun, public hols
- 🍽 Theatre café (£) opposite
- ℹ Avenida Arriaga 16
- ♿ Few
- 💷 Moderate
- ↔ Jardim de Santa Catarina (➤ 57), Museu Fortaleza (➤ 53)

No visit to Madeira is complete without sampling the island's famous wine

31

Funchal's Jardim Botânico

INFORMATION

➕ Off d1

✉ Quinta do Bom Sucesso, Caminho do Meio

☎ 211 200

🕐 Daily 9–6. Closed 25 Dec

🍴 Café (£) in grounds

🚌 Town bus 31

♿ Few

🎫 Inexpensive (includes entry to the nearby Jardim dos Loiros, ▶ 57)

Madeira has earned the nickname 'God's botanical garden' thanks to the huge variety of flowers that thrive in its balmy climate. See them displayed in a riot of colour at Funchal's Botanical Garden.

Nineteenth-century writers bestowed many fanciful names on Madeira to describe the island's botanical wealth – 'a floating green-house' and 'God's botanical garden' being among them. The first plant seeds were probably carried by oceanic currents from West Africa, or reached Madeira in bird droppings. Thriving in the island's fertile volcanic soil, species evolved that are unique to the island. Early settlers may have destroyed many more plants as they slashed and burned the dense vegetation. Zarco ordered the island's woods to be set alight, and such was the ferocity of the resulting blaze that the explorers were forced to put out to sea to escape the heat.

Even so, it is unlikely that the whole island was burned, for several large areas of wilderness remain, and the Botanical Garden displays examples of the trees and shrubs that make up Madeira's virgin forest. Among them is the aptly named dragon tree, with its smooth bark and claw-like leaf clusters, valued since ancient times for its red sap used for cloth dyeing.

Competing with the dragon tree are the many strange and colourful plants introduced to Madeira from far-distant lands, all displayed here in a series of terraced beds. Stars of the show include the tropical orchids (in flower from November to March), while other beds are devoted to the plants that underpin Madeira's cut-flower trade – such as bird of paradise plants and arum lilies – and a fine collection of cacti and sculptural agaves.

The geometrically designed cacti garden

Funchal's Mercado dos Lavradores

The covered market in Funchal is a cornucopia of colourful island produce, a great place to shop for fruit, flowers and souvenirs. If you don't want to buy, just come here to enjoy the bustle.

The Mercado dos Lavradores (Workers' Market) was built in the 1930s as a producers' market, where island farmers and fishermen could bring their produce for sale direct to the public. Now professional retailers predominate, but the original spirit prevails on Friday, as farmers from the remotest corners of Madeira descend on Funchal in loaded-down pick-up trucks.

Flower-sellers in traditional island costume have colonised the entrance to the market. Their stalls sell keenly priced cut flowers and bulbs – tubs full of amaryllis bulbs, freshly dug and smelling of earth, or delicate orchid blooms might tempt you to buy a souvenir of the island's horticultural richness.

In the fish hall, there are scenes to turn the stomach. If the razor-sharp teeth and large staring eyes of the scabbard fish do not give you nightmares, the sight of huge tuna fish being gutted and filleted may well.

For more pleasant sights and fragrances, head for the upper floor, with its lavish displays of seasonal fruit and vegetables. The stallholders will seek to convince you that their fruits are the best by proffering a free sample on the end of a long knife. If you are self-catering on Madeira, you could do worse than come here to buy good fresh food, and if you are not, then just come here to experience the atmosphere.

INFORMATION

- ✚ c2
- ✉ Rua Dr Fernão Ornelas
- 🕐 Mon–Thu 7–4; Fri 7–8; Sat 7–3. Closed Sun
- 🍴 Many stalls selling snacks, plus bars and pavement cafés in the nearby Zona Velha
- ♿ None
- ↔ Zona Velha (➤ 30)

Head for the market's upper floor for fresh fruit and vegetables

33

Funchal's Museu de Arte Sacra

✚ b2
✉ Rua do Bispo 21
☎ 228 900
🕐 Tue–Sat 10–12:30, 2–5:30;
Sun 10–1. Closed Mon,
public hols

Enjoy masterpieces of Flemish art, paid for by Madeira's highly profitable sugar trade with northern Europe.

Funchal's Sacred Art Museum is housed in the former bishop's palace, built in 1600 and given its gracious cobbled courtyard and entrance staircase when the building was remodelled between 1748 and 1757. Displayed on the first floor is a collection of ancient religious vestments, silverware and statuary collected from remote churches all over Madeira. Some of these objects date to the earliest years of the island's colonisation, including the intricately decorated processional cross donated to Funchal Cathedral by the Portuguese King Manuel I, who reigned from 1490 to 1520.

The best of the museum's treasures are displayed on the upper floor. Here you can enjoy the naturalism and human pathos of several beautiful painted wooden statues of the Virgin and Child, as well as the warm colours of several fine Flemish masterpieces. For many years it was not known who painted these remarkable pictures of the Nativity, the Crucifixion and of various saints. By comparison with works by known artists, scholars have now deduced that they are principally the work of leading painters based in Bruges and Antwerp in the late 15th and early 16th centuries, including Gerard David (1468–1523), Dieric Bouts (died 1475) and Jan Provost (1465–1529). Several paintings include portraits of the donors, wealthy merchants who made a fortune from the Madeiran sugar trade. One fine example shows an Italian merchant, Simon Acciaiuoli, kneeling at prayer with his Scottish wife, Mary Drummond, in a painting of the Descent from the Cross, while another shows Simon Gonçalves da Câmara, the grandson of Zarco, Madeira's discoverer, and his family.

Top: *Madeira's 'white gold' (sugar trade) paid for this Flemish portrait of St Peter*
Above: *The* Machico Adoration *depicts Madeiran landowners and merchants*

Funchal's Museu Freitas

The stately rooms in this balconied town house provide glimpses into life on Madeira over the last 150 years.

INFORMATION

✚ a2

✉ Calçada de Santa Clara

☎ 220 578

🕐 Tue–Sat 10–12:30, 2–6. Closed Sun, Mon, public hols

♿ Few

💰 Moderate

Convento de Santa Clara (➤ 55),
Museu Municipal (➤ 53)

The Museu Freitas sits halfway up the steep and cobbled Calçada de Santa Clara, near the Convento de Santa Clara (➤ 55).

The first part of the museum consists of a newly built gallery covering the history of *azulejos* tiles, those brightly coloured ceramics that decorate church walls all over Madeira, as well as domestic homes. Originating in the Islamic east, the practice of using tiles spread from Persia to Portugal via Moorish North Africa and Spain. Madeira lacked suitable clays to produce its own tiles and so imported them from Seville in the 16th century, and later from the Netherlands. Examples of tiles from the Convento de Santa Clara are among the earliest exhibits, while the last flowering of tile manufacture includes some lovely art-nouveau designs.

The second part of the museum consists of the house bequeathed to Funchal by the lawyer Dr Frederico de Freitas in 1978. The rambling mansion dates back to the late 17th century, when it was built by the Count of Calçada. Art-nouveau furnishings, a pretty conservatory in the garden and a glass-roofed winter garden all lend charm to a house crammed with fascinating objects collected by Dr Freitas during the course

of his travels around the world – including more than 2,000 jugs. The collections include oriental carpets, religious paintings, *azulejos* and fine antique furnishings, as well as 17th- and 18th-century hand-carved and painted crib figures originating from mainland Portugal and the Portuguese colonies of Goa and Macau.

Top: *a watercolour by Isabella de Franca*
Above: *a mosaic floor in the courtyard of the art-nouveau conservatory*

Funchal's Quinta das Cruzes

INFORMATION

➕ a1

✉ Calçada do Pico 1

☎ 741 382

🕐 Tue–Sat 10–12:30, 2–5:30;
Sun 10–1. Closed Mon,
public hols

♿ Few

💲 Moderate

🔄 Convento de Santa Clara
(➤ 55)

The 'Mansion of the Crosses' was built for its wealthy owners in the 18th century and is now a showcase for Madeira's art and architecture.

Of the many fine mansions built by wealthy merchants around Funchal, the Quinta das Cruzes is the only one open to the public. Zarco, the discoverer of Madeira and the island's first governor, built his house on this site in the 1450s, but little remains from this era except for some architectural fragments displayed in the gardens. These include gravestones, crosses and broken pieces of church fonts, as well as all that remains of Funchal's pillory, where miscreants were once publicly flogged. Most striking of all are two stone window frames, carved with dancing figures and man-eating lions in the style known as Manueline, after the reigning monarch.

The present house dates from the 18th century, when it was built for the Lomelino family, wealthy wine merchants from Genova. Furnished in the Empire style that was popular at the time, the rooms are arranged thematically, with areas devoted to oriental art, French porcelain, topographical views and portraits, costume and crib figures.

The basement contains an unusual collection of furniture made from recycled packing cases. Sugar was once so precious that it was shipped in chests made from best Brazilian satinwood. Once competition from the New World destroyed Madeira's sugar trade, enterprising cabinet makers reused the wood to make the fine cupboards displayed here.

The bright façade of the Quinta das Cruzes

Funchal's Sé

Founded in 1485 on the command of the King, Funchal's cathedral is one of Madeira's oldest buildings and a link with the island's original settlers.

Portugal's King Manuel I was so proud of his newly acquired island province that he decided to send one of Lisbon's top architects, Pedro Enes, to build a new cathedral for Funchal. The result, completed in 1514, is essentially a sombre building, although it is enlivened with Arabic-style architectural details. The most lavish exterior decoration is found not around the entrance portal, as is customary, but at the east end of the church, where the roofline is decorated with pinnacles shaped like miniature minarets. These echo the shape of the spire, which is covered in glazed *azulejos* (tiles) originally intended to protect the structure from wind and rain, rather than act as decoration. The comparatively plain portal bears King Manuel I's coat of arms, incorporating the red cross of the Knights Templar, of which Manuel was Grand Master.

The cool interior of the cathedral reveals its secrets slowly, as your eyes adapt to the darkness. High above the nave is a carved wooden ceiling inlaid with geometric designs in ivory. If you look long enough you will begin to make out strange animals and exotic flowers among the designs. Easier to appreciate are the choir stalls, boldly carved with near-lifesize figures of the Apostles, painted in gold against a background of powder blue. The Apostles are dressed in stylish hats, cloaks, tunics, boots and belts, giving us a good idea of the clothes worn by prosperous Madeiran sugar merchants when the stalls were carved in the early 16th century. More entertaining scenes from contemporary life are found carved on the undersides of the choir seats. As well as cherubs, there are monkeys and pigs and a porter carrying a pigskin full of wine.

INFORMATION

- ✚ b2
- ✉ Largo da Sé
- ☎ 228 155
- 🕐 Daily 9–12:30, 4–5:30 (with services early morning and early evening)
- 🍽 Many pavement cafés (£) on the cathedral square
- ♿ Few
- 🎫 Free
- 🔁 Museu de Arte Sacra (➤ 34)

A line of saints under elaborate gilded canopies on the choir stalls

Machico

INFORMATION

➕ E3

✉ 24km northeast of Funchal

🍴 Several cafés and restaurants in Rua do Mercado (Market Street), including the Mercado Velha restaurant (£, ☎ 962 370) and the Pastelaria Galã café (£, ☎ 965 720)

🚌 Buses 20, 23, 53, 78, 113, 156

❓ Festa di Santissimo Sacramento (Feast of the Holy Sacrament), celebrated on the last weekend in Aug; procession in honour of Our Lord of Miracles 8–9 Oct

ℹ Forte de Nossa Senhora do Amparo (☎ 962 289, ⏰ Mon–Fri 9–12:30, 2–5; Sat 9–12)

♿ Few

↔ Prainha (▶ 58)

This is where Zarco first set foot on Madeira in 1420, claiming for Portugal an island that had been known to sailors for thousands of years.

Among those who got to Madeira before Zarco were Robert Machin and Anne of Hereford, shipwrecked here after their storm-tossed ship was driven out into the Atlantic from the coast of Portugal. Robert and Anne died within days of each other and were buried by the rest of the crew, who later escaped by building a raft. On finding their graves some 50 years later, Zarco is said to have named the spot Machico, in Machin's honour (in fact, it is more likely that Machico is a corruption of Monchique, Zarco's home town in Portugal).

Zarco and his fellow navigator, Tristão Vaz Teixeira, were appointed governors of Madeira in 1425, with Zarco ruling the west from Funchal, and Teixeira in charge of the east, based in Machico. It is his statue that stands in front of the town's 15th-century parish church.

The smaller Capela dos Milagres (Chapel of the Miracles), to the east of the town, is reputed to be built on the site of Machin's grave. The original church was washed away by floods in 1803, but the Gothic crucifix was found floating at sea and returned by an American sailor.

Machico's third church (now locked and derelict) was built in 1739 to honour São Roque after he was believed to have answered the townspeople's prayers and saved them from plague. It stands on the western arm of Machico's wide bay, beyond the fish market and the triangular fortress, built in 1706, which has been restored to house the town's tourist office.

Some visitors may find Machico a gritty town, surrounded as it is by light industry, but it has an attractive historic centre, with cobbled streets and pleasant squares.

Monte

High above the capital, the hill town of Monte is now easily reached thanks to the cable car that runs from Funchal's Zona Velha.

Quite apart from the cable car (▶ 48) and the famous Monte Toboggan Ride (▶ 40), there are several good reasons for coming to Monte. One is to visit the Church of Nossa Senhora (Our Lady), whose spotlit façade is a prominent landmark at night, visible on the hillside high above Funchal. The classical building, its grey basalt detailing contrasted with whitewashed walls, is reached by climbing a steep flight of 74 stone steps. Penitents scramble up these steps on their knees during the Feast of the Assumption. Inside the church is a precious statue of the Virgin housed in a silver tabernacle. It is said the 15th-century statue was given to a Madeiran shepherd girl by the Virgin herself, and it is credited with many miracles. The north chapel contains the imposing black coffin of the Emperor Charles I, who died of pneumonia on Madeira in 1922, aged 35.

At the foot of the church steps is a stretch of cobbled road marking the start of the Monte Toboggan Ride.

The luxuriant Jardim do Monte municipal garden stands to the north of the steps, built around a short stretch of railway viaduct, now smothered in tropical greenery. The viaduct is a vestige of the rack-and-pinion railway that once linked Monte to Funchal. The railway opened in 1894 but was closed after an accident in 1939, when an engine blew up, killing four people. The station building survives on the main square above, the Largo do Fonte, where an ancient plane tree shelters waiting taxi drivers.

In the opposite direction, it is a short walk to the Monte Palace Tropical Garden (pictured above), 7ha of lush hillside with fishponds, fountains, grottoes and Japanese-style gates.

INFORMATION

- 🞢 D3/4
- ✉ 6km north of Funchal
- 🍴 Café (£) on main square, and café/restaurant (££) in the Monte Palace Tropical Garden
- 🚌 20, 21 (or the cable car, ▶ 48)
- ♿ Few
- ↔ Terreiro da Luta (▶ 55)
- ❓ The Feast of the Assumption, 15 Aug; religious ceremonies, fireworks and feasting

Monte Palace Tropical Garden

- ✉ Caminho do Monte 174
- ☎ 782 339/742 650
- 🕐 Mon–Sat 9–6. (Call to confirm times on Sun)

The Church of Nossa Senhora do Monte

39

Monte Toboggan Ride

+ D3/4
- Toboggan rides start from the foot of the steps of Nossa Senhora do Monte church
- Toboggan rides are available daily, 9–dusk
- Café (£) frequented by toboggan drivers alongside church steps
- Town bus 20 or the cable car (➤ 48)
- Expensive
- Monte (➤ 39)

The quintessential Madeira experience is to slide in a metal-shod toboggan down the steep cobbled streets linking Monte to Funchal.

Was Ernest Hemingway being ironic when he described the Monte Toboggan Ride as one of the most exhilarating experiences of his life? The only way to find out is to try it for yourself by heading up to the hill town of Monte, high above Funchal. Here you can join the line of apprehensive travellers queuing to slide back down to the capital in a wicker basket mounted on polished metal runners. The ride starts at the foot of the steps of the Nossa Senhora do Monte church, where you will see the drivers hanging about in their uniform of white shirt and trousers and straw hat. Two drivers, wearing rubber-soled boots for grip, will push and steer you over the bumpy cobbles and ensure that you do not come to grief as you negotiate sharp bends.

The 4km trip to Funchal will last about 20 minutes (for a shorter ride, you can take the 10-minute trip to Livramento). Some visitors consider this brief but unique journey to be the highlight of their visit to Madeira – others consider it overpriced hype (as well as the price of the ride, you will be expected to tip the toboggan drivers, and pay for the souvenir photographs that are taken as you descend and presented to you at the journey's end).

Hold on for a thrilling and unusual ride!

Pico do Arieiro

Drive to the top of Madeira's third-highest peak for raw volcanic landscapes and spectacular views, best enjoyed at sunset or sunrise.

Pico do Arieiro, 1,818m high, is easily reached from central Funchal by driving north on the EN 103 road to the Poiso Pass, and then taking the EN 202 west.

As you climb, the green woodland that cloaks much of central Madeira gives way to a wilder upland landscape of sheep-grazed turf. The sense of travelling to a different world is reinforced by the cloud belt, which hangs at around 1,200m. Passing through this miasma of swirling mist and driving rain, you will emerge in brilliant sunshine. Bare rock soon becomes the predominant feature in the landscape, and only the hardiest of plants can find any toehold among the clinker-like tufa that makes up the summit of Pico do Arieiro.

To compensate for the lack of vegetation, there are tremendous views over an endless succession of knife-edge ridges and sheer cliffs. Cotton-wool clouds hang in the valleys far below and the only sound comes from the wind. The predominant colours are purple, burnt orange and chocolate brown, a reminder of Madeira's volcanic origins. The rocks are even more vividly colourful when lit by the red and orange rays of the setting sun, or the pink light of dawn.

A 6km path links Pico do Arieiro with Pico Ruivo (Madeira's highest peak), but don't go beyond the first gate if you are scared of heights. After this the path runs along an unfenced ridge, with vertigo-inducing drops either side. The path can be slippery and there are five tunnels along the route.

INFORMATION

+ D3

🍴 Restaurant (££) and snack bar (£) in the Pousada do Pico do Arieiro Hotel on the summit

❓ You can stay at Pousada do Pico do Arieiro (► 74), an 18-room government-run hotel at the summit (☎ 230 110)

Hill walkers on the track near the summit

Pico Ruivo

INFORMATION

Walk:

Distance 5km

Time 2 hours up and back, plus time to rest and admire the views

Start/end point Achada do Teixeira rest house

⊞ D2

🍴 A rest house near the summit sells drinks and chocolate, but it is not always open

🚗 Taxi/hire car required

❓ Carry a light jacket as it can be cold on the mountain top

Stand on top of Madeira's highest mountain and you will be rewarded with breathtaking views of the central mountain range, and of the island of Porto Santo floating in the sea.

The climb to the 1,861m summit of Pico Ruivo may leave you giddy and breathless, but you will feel on top of the world as you take in the panoramic views.

There is no shelter along the route, so wear suitable clothing to protect yourself from over-exposure to the sun and wind. Take water and food, and start early, as clouds build up from around 10:30 onwards and obscure the views.

To reach the path up the mountain, drive eastwards from Santana along the EN 101, then turn off south onto the road signposted to Pico Ruivo. Carry on for 10km to the car park and rest house at Achada do Teixeira. From the car park there is only one track, and it goes up – steeply at first but soon levelling out to a gentle climb, with views across the volcanic landscape of Madeira's central mountain range. The path passes through sheep-grazed meadows then up through woodland, where huge, gnarled heaths line the route.

After 45 minutes, the path divides; take the path to the right up through a gate and on to the government rest house, a prominent white building. Two minutes on, the path divides and you take the left fork. It is a steep scramble from here up through the purple-red tufas that give the Pico Ruivo (Red Peak) its name. It is worth the effort for the views when you finally reach the top.

Back at the car park, admire the rock formation called Homem em Pé (Standing Man). Madeiran children are told that this great lump of volcanic basalt is a giant turned into stone – it is actually a volcanic dyke, a sheet of lava intruded upwards through a crack in the volcano's side.

Porto Santo

Porto Santo is all about sun, sea and sand, and almost nothing else. One of the chief attractions is that its magnificent sweep of beach remains clean, unspoilt and undeveloped.

Porto Santo's population of 5,000 earns much of its living during July and August, when a steady stream of visitors arrives to soak up the sun and dance the night away in hotel discos.

Some people take the relatively expensive 15-minute flight from Madeira, while most risk seasickness on the catamaran that makes the 90-minute journey across the 37km of choppy ocean separating the two islands.

Vila Baleira is Porto Santo's capital, and it is here that most of the island's inhabitants live. The town was founded by Bartolomeu Perestrelo, the island's first governor. In the 15th century it was a profitable colony, producing cereals, wines and sugar, as well as dyestuffs from the sap of dragon trees.

Two dragon trees survive in the town's main square, Largo do Pelourinho, flanking the entrance to the 16th-century Town Hall. Alongside is the popular Bar Gel Burger, the centre of the island's social life. To the north is the much-restored parish church, with only a small side chapel surviving from the 15th-century Gothic original. Behind the church is the Casa Museu Cristóvão Colombo (➤ 60).

From opposite the Town Hall, Rua Infante D Henrique, the town's palm-lined main street, leads straight to the beach.

Other attractions on the island include the Fonte da Areia (Spring in the Sand), whose water is rumoured to restore body and soul (➤ 60), and the Serra de Dentro Valley, 5km northeast of Vila Baleira, which looks like the setting for a Wild West movie.

INFORMATION

➕ Island map on inside back cover

Vila Baleira

✉ On the southern coast of Porto Santo, 10 minutes' drive from the airport

🍴 The Baiana café (£, ☎ 984 649), on Largo do Pelourinho, serves excellent grilled fish

♿ Few

🛈 Rua Dr Vieira da Castro (☎ 982 361)

🔁 For a walk along the sands of Porto Santo ➤ 17. For more Porto Santo attractions ➤ 60

Diving with a shoal of tuna in the waters off Porto Santo

43

Quinta do Palheiro Ferreiro

INFORMATION

+ D4
✉ Palheiro Ferreiro, 8km east of Funchal
☎ 793 044
🕐 Mon–Fri 9:30–12:30. Closed Sat, Sun, 1 Jan, Easter, 1 May, 25 Dec
🚌 Town bus 37
♿ Few
💷 Moderate

The botanical riches of Africa, Asia and the Americas are combined in the beautifully landscaped gardens of this aristocratic estate.

Of all the gardens on Madeira, those surrounding the Quinta do Palheiro Ferreiro (also known as Blandy's Gardens) are the most rewarding. Here the spirit of the English garden has been transposed to Madeira, where full advantage has been taken of the frost-free environment. Plants that would curl up and die further north, or which have to be cosseted in the hothouse, thrive here out of doors. To create this lovely garden, successive generations of the Blandy family have been able to draw on the limitless treasures of the botanical world, planting gorgeous proteas from southern Africa, flame-flowered climbers from southern America, sweetly scented Japanese flowering shrubs, and Chinese trees with exotically patterned bark. The result is a garden full of surprises and unexpected plant combinations.

The English influence is evident in the division of the garden into a series of 'rooms' divided by hedges and linked by mixed borders. Smaller intimate areas, such as the peaceful and shady Ladies' Garden, with its topiary peacocks, give way to more open areas, such as the sweeping lawns surrounding the baroque chapel built by the Count of Carvalhal. The wealthy count was the original owner of this aristocratic estate, which the Blandy family acquired in 1885. Part of the estate remains exactly as the count laid it out in the late 18th century, including the stately avenue of gnarled old plane trees that leads up to his original mansion. Beyond the mansion is an extensive area of informal woodland, signposted 'Inferno' (Hell), where blue morning glory vines trail among primeval tree ferns from New Zealand.

A water lily in the sunken garden

Ribeira Brava

To understand why Ribeira Brava (Wild River) is so named, you have to visit in winter, when the river running through the town is in full spate.

During most of the year Ribeira Brava's river belies its true nature. Over several thousand millennia this river has carved out a deep cleft that seems almost to divide Madeira in two, running due north from Ribeira Brava up to the Encumeada Pass and on to São Vicente, on the north coast of Madeira. The road that runs up this valley has long been an important transport route, which is why Ribeira Brava has grown into a sizeable town, with a market and a number of seafront cafés where farmers, taking their produce to Funchal, stop to break their journey.

Located just back from the seafront is the splendid Church of São Bento (St Benedict). Like most churches on Madeira it has been rebuilt many times, but there are several features remaining from the original 15th-century church, including the painted font, decorated with grapes, pomegranates and wild beasts, and the carved stone pulpit. The right-hand chapel contains a fine Flemish painting of the Nativity, surrounded by gilded woodwork.

At the north end of town, the new Museu Etnográfico da Madeira (Madeira Ethnographic Museum) offers displays on fishing, agriculture, weaving and wine-making.

Ribeira Brava is the starting point for exploring the western third of Madeira, but the drive to the town alone used to take more than an hour from Funchal. However, in 1997 transport on the island was revolutionised with the opening of the Via Rápida expressway, so the town is now only 20 minutes away.

INFORMATION

- ✚ C4
- ✉ 32km west of Funchal
- 🍴 Good choice of cafés and restaurants (£–££) along the seafront road, and along the cobbled main street, Rua do Visconde
- 🚌 Bus 7
- ♿ None
- ↔ Boca da Encumeada (➤ 24)
- ℹ Tourist office (☎ 951 675) in the Forte de São Bento, along the seafront road

Museu Etnográfico da Madeira
- ✉ Rua de São Francisco 24
- ☎ 952 598
- 🕐 Tue–Sun 10–12:30, 2–6

The church of São Bento

Ribeiro Frio

INFORMATION

- ✚ D3
- ✉ 14km north of Funchal
- 🍴 Victor's Bar (££, ☎ 575 898), alongside the trout farm
- 🚌 Buses 103, 138
- ↔ Pico do Arieiro (▶ 41)

Ribeiro Frio is a valley paradise, where Nature's attractions have been enhanced by plantings of azaleas, tree ferns and camellias.

Ribeiro Frio is a delightful spot set among scented woodland. Here the fresh clean waters of the Ribeiro Frio (meaning 'cold river') are channelled into a series of deep pools to create a small trout farm. Trout inevitably features on the menu of the restaurant alongside. Woodland glades on the opposite side of the road are planted with flowering trees and shrubs to create a miniature botanical garden, where basking butterflies add to the colour.

Trout circle in the green waters of the Ribeiro Frio Trout Farm

Ribeiro Frio is the meeting point of several *levada* walks. One of the easiest is the walk to Balcões, which you can pick up by walking downhill from the trout farm and taking the broad track to the left that leads to the *levada*. Follow the wide level path for about 15 minutes to reach Balcões, whose name (meaning 'balcony') becomes obvious when you arrive: stunning landscapes open up from this hillside viewpoint across the sun-dappled Ametade Valley to the Penha de Águia (Eagle Rock), on Madeira's northern coast. The *levada* continues for another 2km, with views of the bare volcanic peaks around Pico do Arieiro (▶ 41). On the opposite side of the road is the Levada do Furado, signposted to Portela. If you walk as far as the bridge over the River Bezerro (allow an hour) you will experience a sequence of splendid views across central Madeira's mountainous green interior.

Santana

Santana has put itself on the tourist map as *the* place to see Madeira's unique triangular houses, with their thatched roofs and colourful walls.

Santana presents a picture of domestic and agricultural prosperity. Here the predominant colours are the greens of terraced fields and hay meadows, interspersed by apple, pear and cherry orchards. Dotted among the haystacks and the pollarded willows are triangular thatched buildings, used by local farmers as cow byres. Here cattle are tethered for their own safety (to prevent them from tumbling on the steep hillsides), and to provide them with cool shade in summer and shelter from winter's wind.

Traditionally, people have lived in these ingenious structures too. Many are neglected and decaying, but a government scheme to encourage their restoration means that several in Santana are still inhabited. With their brightly painted triangular façades and a roof that sweeps from the ridge to the ground, these A-framed buildings are highly distinctive. They are also surprisingly spacious, as you will discover if you visit the souvenir shop in the centre of Santana, where a typical A-frame house, called a *palheiro*, has been faithfully restored.

The EN 101-5 road south leads to Achada do Teixeira, from where you can walk to Pico Ruivo (➤ 42), Madeira's highest peak. Further north a rough minor road leads to the government rest house at Queimadas. This marks the start of one of Madeira's finest *levada* walks, taking in spectacular ravines and primeval forest. The ultimate goal (reached after about an hour) is the 300m-high waterfall that cascades into the pool at the bottom of the well-named fern- and moss-filled Caldeirão Verde (Green Cauldron).

INFORMATION

+ D2
✉ Santana lies 42km north of Funchal
🍴 Several cafés and restaurants (£–££)
🚌 Buses 103, 132, 138
♿ None
💵 Free
↔ Pico Ruivo (➤ 42)

A Madeiran palheiro

47

Teleféricos da Madeira

INFORMATION

➕ c2; D3/4
✉ Avenida das Comunidades
   Madeirenses, Funchal;
   Caminho das Babosas 8,
   Monte
☎ 780 280
🕐 Summer: daily 9–8:30.
   Winter: daily 9–6
🎫 Expensive

The journey on the Madeira Cable Car is as thrilling as a theme-park ride – if you dare to open your eyes you will be treated to a bird's eye view of Funchal.

The Madeira Cable Car revolutionised island transport when it opened in autumn 2000, providing a new and exciting way of travelling from Funchal to the pretty hill town of Monte. Courtesy of Austrian technology, you can now sail high above the rooftops of the capital, in cars carrying up to eight passengers. The 15-minute ride starts in an ultra-modern glass and steel building near the promenade at the Zona Velha (Old Town). From here you are whisked upwards, with intimate aerial views of Funchal's numerous hidden gardens and patios. The cable car then sails over the canyon-like valley of the João Gomes river, and finally lands you back on terra firma in Monte, set on the slopes of Pico Alto, some 5km north of the capital.

Monte offers a great range of diversions (▶ 39). To reach the centre of the village, turn left out of the cable-car station.

Competition from the cable car has driven down the price of the famous Monte Toboggan Ride (▶ 40), so you might want to return to Funchal using this unusual mode of transport.

The Madeira Cable Car offers panoramic views of Funchal and its harbour

MADEIRA's
best

ÃO GONÇALVES
ZARCO

49

Towns and Villages

The statue of Christ at Garajau is similar to the larger statue at Rio de Janeiro

CALHETA

Calheta is the main town for the southwestern coast, a fertile sunbathed region where the orange-roofed houses are lost among a sea of banana, grapevine and sugar-cane plantations. If you come here on 7 or 8 September even the streets are covered in flowers as carpets of blooms are laid out to celebrate the Feast of Our Lady of Loreto. The town's church contains a large tabernacle of ebony and silver, donated by Portugal's King Manuel I (1469–1521). The sweet smell of cane syrup from the factory next door to the church may tempt you to take a tour to watch rum and molasses being produced.

➕ B3 ✉ South coast, 61km west of Funchal ☎ Sugar mill: 822 264 🍴 Marisqueria do Camarão 🚌 80, 115, 139, 142 ♿ None

GARAJAU

Garajau is Portuguese for 'tern', and the village is named after the attractive black-headed sea birds that nest on the nearby cliffs. Garajau's most prominent landmark is the huge statue of Christ, erected here in 1927. From the statue you can walk down a cobbled track leading to the base of the cliffs, where a concrete causeway links a number of small boulder-strewn coves and beaches.

➕ E4 ✉ 8km east of Funchal 🍴 Snack Bar O Neptuno 🚌 2, 109, 110, 155 ♿ Few

PONTA DO SOL

Sunset is a good time to visit Ponta do Sol for uninterrupted views of fireworks in the western sky while strolling along the harbour promenade or enjoying an ice cream at the ornate seafront kiosk. Steep cobbled streets lead up to the church, with its unusual green ceramic font, donated by King Manuel I (1469–1521), and its ancient wooden ceilings, painted with scenes from the Life of the Virgin.

➕ B3 ✉ 42km west of Funchal 🍴 Beachside bar (£) in Ponta do Sol; try also the A Poita restaurant (££, ☎ 974 871) in Madalena do Mar for fish soup and seafood 🚌 4 ♿ None

PORTO DA CRUZ

Porto da Cruz was once an important harbour town, declining into a quiet backwater once road transport took over from boats. It is reached by following the road that skirts the small fortress-crowned hill to the east of the village, past the sandy beach and the sugar mill and distillery. A sweet toffee-like scent fills the air during the sugar-harvesting season – March to May – when production of *aguardente*, a rum-like spirit made from crushed sugar cane, is under way. To the west, the Penha de Águia (Eagle Rock) rises to a height of 590m, casting shadows over the village.

🔢 E2 ✉ 30km northeast of Funchal 🚌 53, 78, 103 ♿ Few

PORTO DO MONIZ

Porto do Moniz is a surprisingly cosmopolitan place for a village located at the northernmost extremity of Madeira, thanks to the waterfront hotel catering for travellers on round-the-island tours. The sea-water bathing area in front of the hotel is popular. Nearby, the Atlantic waves that crash against Madeira's northern shore carry salt-laden spray far up into the surrounding hills, hence the ingenious use of grass and bracken fences to protect the crops.

🔢 B1 ✉ 75km northwest of Funchal 🍴 Choice of restaurants (££), including the Cachalote (☎ 853 180) 🚌 80, 139 ♿ None

SANTA CRUZ

The people of Santa Cruz get an intimate view of aeroplanes coming in to land at nearby Santa Catarina airport, but the town retains the peaceful atmosphere of a bygone era. The parish church of 1479 is one of the oldest on the island and may have shared the same architect as Funchal's cathedral. There is also a small art gallery in the library, a market, a beach and the Palm Beach lido. Flowering trees fill the park surrounding the 19th-century Law Court, while date palms and dragon trees line the seafront road.

🔢 E3 ✉ 17km east of Funchal 🍴 Cafés along the seafront (£) serving homemade cakes 🚌 20, 23, 53, 78, 113, 156 ♿ Few

SÃO VICENTE

São Vicente is a prosperous agricultural town, with hotels and cafés catering to travellers exploring the northern coast. The historic core has traffic-free cobbled streets lined with shops to tempt visitors, tubs brimming with flowers and houses painted a dazzling white under orange roof tiles. In the 17th-century church, the painted ceiling shows St Vincent blessing the town, and the same saint appears on the elaborately carved and gilded altar, blessing a ship.

🔢 C2 ✉ 55km north of Funchal 🍴 Choice of cafés/restaurants (£–££), including O Virgilio (££) 🚌 4, 80, 132, 139 ♿ None

A bird's eye view of Porto Moniz

51

Museums

FORTALEZA DE SÃO TIAGO

Built in 1614, the Fortress of St James was one of the last fortifications to be completed on Madeira. Newly restored, it now houses a museum of contemporary art, but the rather unexciting works on display are a distraction from the real interest of the fortress – the maze of passages, staircases and towers that make a perfect playground for children, and the views over the rooftops of Funchal to be had from the ramparts.

➕ d2 ✉ Rua do Portão de São Tiago, Funchal
☎ 226 456 🕐 Mon–Sat 10–12:30, 2–5:30. Closed Sun, public hols ♿ Few 💷 Moderate

Fortaleza de São Tiago now houses an art museum

IBTAM HANDICRAFTS INSTITUTE

IBTAM is the body that oversees standards in Madeira's economically important embroidery industry, and the small museum in its headquarters building is a showcase for Madeiran handicrafts. The rather drab, old-fashioned displays are brought to life by the vibrant colours of traditional island costume. Displayed on the staircase leading up to the museum is an impressive 7-million-stitch tapestry depicting a flower-filled Madeiran landscape, made in 1958–61.

➕ c1 ✉ Rua do Visconde de Anadia 44, Funchal ☎ 223 141
🕐 Mon–Fri 10–12:30, 2:30–5:30. Closed Sat, Sun, public hols
♿ Few 💷 Moderate

UNDER SIEGE

Attracted by stories of Madeira's massive sugar-derived wealth, French, English, Algerian and Turkish pirates regularly attacked Funchal from the 16th century, looting churches and wine cellars and killing anyone who stood in their way. In response, Madeira's governor ordered the construction of massive walls and fortifications, which were extended and reinforced over a 100-year period.

MUSEU 'A CIDADE DO AÇÚCAR'

This museum is constructed around the excavated remains of a house built in 1495 for Jeanin Esmerandt, a Flemish merchant working for the Bruges-based Company Despars. Christopher Columbus twice stayed in the house as a guest of Esmerandt: in 1480, and again in 1498 (after his pioneering voyage across to the Americas). The house was demolished in 1876 and excavated in 1989. Finds from the excavation exhibited here include pottery, food remains, coins, jewellery and bone buttons. Also on display are ceramic sugar cones, similar to those that feature on Funchal's coat of arms, and 16th-century engravings of the sugar-making process. The great wealth that sugar brought to Funchal is represented by religious paintings and statues acquired by the city's merchants.

➕ c2 ✉ Praça do Colombo, Funchal ☎ 236 910 🕐 Tue–Fri 9–12:30, 2–5:30. Closed public hols ♿ Few 💷 Moderate

MUSEU FORTALEZA

Housed within the bastions of the Palaçio de São
Lourenço (Palace of St Lawrence), the Fortress
Museum is only open to those who ring in advance
and book a place on the guided tour. Tours take in
the grand rooms installed when the fortress was
converted to a palace for the military and civilian
governors of Madeira in the 19th century. Also on
display are historic weapons. The fortress was still
incomplete in 1566, when Bertrand de Montluc, the
French pirate, raided Madeira, rounded up 250 of the
most prominent citizens and put them to the sword
within the fortress walls. Now it is classified as a
national monument and is one of Portugal's best-
preserved early fortifications. If you don't want to go
on a tour, you can at least look at the fortress's 16th-
century carved stone gateway, off Avenida Arriaga.

➕ b2 ✉ Praça do Colombo, Funchal ☎ 202 530 ◷ Wed, Fri, by
guided tour at 10:30 and 3 ♿ Few 🎫 Moderate

MUSEU FRANCO

This quiet and little-visited museum celebrates the
artistic achievements of two brothers born on
Madeira but who achieved fame on the wider
European stage. Henrique Franco (1883–1961) was a
painter and his older brother Francisco (1855–1955)
was a sculptor. Both studied in Paris, where they were
friendly with Picasso, Degas and Modigliani, but
their careers were largely centred on the Portuguese
capital, Lisbon. The first part of the museum is
devoted to a series of Gauginesque portraits, painted
by Henrique, while the second part displays
Francisco's vigorous but monochrome sculptures.

➕ c1 ✉ Rua do Bom Jesus 13, Funchal ☎ 230 633 ◷ 10–12:30,
2–5:30. Closed public hols ♿ Few 🎫 Moderate

*A painting by Henrique
Franco, displayed in the
Museu Franco*

MUSEU MUNICIPAL

The Municipal Museum is one of the few
on Madeira that children genuinely enjoy,
thanks to the aquarium on the ground
floor. This is stocked with fish typically
caught off Madeiran shores, including
morose-looking grouper fish, hungry-eyed
moray eels and bottom-dwelling flounders.
Upstairs, there is a collection of stuffed
birds and animals, including sharks with
gaping jaws and giant crabs with metre-
long claws. Displays of typical Madeiran
birds are as close as you are likely to get to
the more elusive species that nest on inaccessible
cliffs.

➕ b2 ✉ Rua da Mouraria 31, Funchal ☎ 229 761 ◷ Tue–Fri
10–6; Sat, Sun, public hols 12–6 ♿ Few 🎫 Moderate

*A sea-bream and a moray
eel in the aquarium of
the Municipal Museum*

53

Viewpoints

A BREATHTAKING DRIVE

The corniche that runs between Porto do Moniz and São Vicente is one of Europe's most spectacular roads, built on a narrow shelf cut into the cliff face high above the raging sea. If you choose to travel it you will need to drive slowly, not only to take in the spectacular coastal views but also to avoid accidents. The road is only one vehicle wide for much of its length so keep an eye open for approaching cars and buses (be warned: when Madeiran drivers flash their lights it means 'I am coming through').

At several points, waterfalls come cascading down on top of your car – Madeirans look on them as a free car wash.

The sheer drop of the cliffs at Ponta de São Lourenço

FAIAL

Faial is worth a stop for the views from the *miradouro* overlooking the Ametade Valley, west of the village.

➕ D2 ✉ 30km north of Funchal 🍴 Casa de Chá do Faial (£, ☎ 572 223) at Lombo do Baixo, south of Faial 🚌 53, 78 ♿ None

PONTA DE SÃO LOURENÇO

Follow the switchback path to the easternmost tip of Madeira and you will feel as if you are standing on the edge of the world. The path gives stunning views of the Ilhas Desertas, inhabited only by seals and birds. Set off from the car park at the easternmost end of the EN 101-3 road. Take the path that starts by the big boulders at the eastern end of the car park. Keep right and head down to the bottom of a shallow valley, then up the other side. After 20 minutes the uphill track meets a boulder wall, with a gap for walkers to pass through. Bear left on a rocky path and descend to the valley where the path splits. Go left to reach a viewpoint high above three purple rocks known as 'seahorses', with views of high cliffs and raging seas. Return to the main path and head left towards the skyline. This will take you to another viewpoint.

➕ F3 **Distance** 2km **Time** 1 hour 30 minutes **Start/end point** Car park at easternmost end of EN 101-3 road, beyond Caniçal

PONTA DO PARGO

Visitors are drawn to the westernmost tip of Madeira by the thought that nothing stands between them and the east coast of America except for hundreds of miles of ocean. Standing alongside the cliff-top lighthouse at Ponta do Pargo, 300m above the sea, you can try spotting fishermen who come here to catch the *pargos* (dolphin fish, no relation to the dolphin) after which Ponta do Pargo (Dolphin Point) is named.

➕ A2 ✉ 77km west of Funchal 🍴 Solar do Pargo café 🚌 142 ♿ None

PAÚL DA SERRA

This windswept high plateau offers expansive views of moorland, although its wild open landscape is now somewhat compromised by a forest of wind turbines. Even so, it is worth coming here to look for wild bilberries in autumn and to savour the eerie atmosphere, or to enjoy the panoramic views to be had when the plateau is not enshrouded in cloud.

➕ B2/3 ✉ 61km northwest of Funchal, either side of the EN 124

Sacred Sites

In the Top 25

CAPELA DOS REIS MAGOS
Inside the Chapel of the Three Kings at Lombo dos Reis is a rare 16th-century reredos, carved in Antwerp with scenes depicting the Adoration of the Magi.
➕ A3 ✉ Between Estreito da Calheta and Jardim do Mar

CONVENTO DE SANTA CLARA
You can take a guided tour of the chapels that lie off these peaceful 15th-century cloisters. They shelter paintings, sculpture and *azulejos*. The nearby church was rebuilt in the 17th century but it stands on the site of a 15th-century chapel where Zarco was buried.
➕ a1 ✉ Calçada de Santa Clara, Funchal ☎ 742 602 🕐 Daily 9–12, 3–6; ring for entry if door is closed 🚻 Few 🎫 Moderate

LORETO CHURCH
The church, built by one of Zarco's daughters-in-law, has a south portal carved in the lively Manueline style of the early 16th century, and a *mudejar*-style ceiling.
➕ B3 ✉ 2km east of Calheta

PONTA DELGADA
The beachside church in Ponta Delgada contains the charred figure of the crucified Christ, which is taken in procession round the village during one of the island's biggest religious festivals, on the first Sunday in September. The figure was found washed up on the shore in the 16th century. In 1908 it survived a fire, which destroyed the rest of the church (now rebuilt).
➕ C1 ✉ 51km north of Funchal 🚌 103 🚻 None

TERREIRO DA LUTA
Terreiro da Luta consists of a massive monument to the Virgin, lit up at night and visible from downtown Funchal. The monument was erected in 1927.
➕ D3 ✉ 8km north of Funchal 🚌 103, 138

THE ZONA VELHA'S CHURCHES
Opposite the lido, in Funchal's Old Town, stands the Igreja do Socorro (also called Santa Maria Maior), rebuilt several times since it was founded in the 16th century in thanksgiving for the ending of an epidemic. By contrast, the tiny Capela do Corpo Santo is a simple 16th-century fishermen's chapel.
➕ d2 ✉ Zona Velha, Funchal

Also worth visiting are the churches in Calheta (➤ 50), Ponta do Sol (➤ 50) and Santa Cruz (➤ 51).

OPENING TIMES

Churches on Madeira are generally open 8–1 and 3–7, but rural churches may be locked outside service times – if so, ask for the key at the next-door house or in a local bar. Alternatively, slip in just before or after the daily service, which usually takes place around 5PM.

The statue of the Virgin Mary at Terreiro da Luta is over 5 metres high

For Children

A girl in traditional Madeiran costume

Madeira has few genuinely child-friendly attractions, so you may need to exercise some imagination to keep your young ones amused. The top attraction in Funchal is the aquarium in the Museu Municipal (► 53). Children who are not afraid of heights will also enjoy the cable car (► 48) – at the end of the ride the Monte Palace Tropical Garden (► 39) will keep them amused for a good hour or more.

BOAT TRIPS

Head for Funchal's yachting marina to see the range of boat trips on offer. Most operators use motor-powered boats, but you can also book excursions on the *Albatroz*, a 20m yacht built in 1939, available for hire with crew for parties of up to 20 people. Trips can be booked through any travel agency, through the tourist office in Funchal or through Turispeca (☎ 231 063) or Costa do Sol (☎ 238 538). An alternative is the *Santa Maria*, a replica of Columbus's ship (☎ 220 327).

DOLPHIN-WATCHING

Teenagers will love this trip, provided they are aware that sighting dolphins is not guaranteed – even so, the boat operators who lead these trips usually know where to look. Two-hour trips take place every Wednesday, departing from Funchal at 10, 1 and 4. Further details from Albatroz Dolphin Watch, Funchal Marina (☎ 223 366).

FOOTBALL

Madeira's first division football team, C S Marítimo, plays home matches on alternate Sunday afternoons in the season. The games are friendly and not marred by crowd violence.
✚ Off map at a2 ✉ Estádio dos Barreiros ☎ Tourist office: 225 658

GRUTAS DE SÃO VICENTE

These caves are popular with children. The only drawback is that the guided tour is so short – you spend only 15–20 minutes inside. The caves are unusual in being created not by water erosion but by molten lava, flowing down from the volcanic peaks of the Paúl da Serra when they last erupted 400,000 years ago. The lava flowed into joints in the rock, melting a tubular path, which visitors now walk along. What appear to be stalactites hanging from the ceiling are drips of molten rock, frozen in situ. The lava flows themselves look just like molten chocolate, hardened into solid rock.
✚ C2 ✉ Sítio do Pé do Passo, São Vicente ☎ 842 404 ⏰ Apr–Sep: 9–9. Oct–Mar: 9–7 ♿ None 🎟 Expensive (children go free)

HELICOPTER TRIPS

If you have money to spare and teenage children to treat, the ultimate in excursions is a helicopter trip over the mountains or along Madeira's scenic coastline. Flights as short as 10 minutes can be arranged through any travel agent or through HeliAtlantis, Estrada da Pontinha, Cais de Contentores (☎ 232 882/4).

JARDIM DOS LOIROS

Exotic screeches, whoops and squawks advertise the presence of this tropical bird garden, where even the brightest flowers are put in the shade by the plumage of cockatoos, parrots, parakeets and macaws. Children will enjoy the antics of the birds, which are displayed in aviaries dotted around the gardens.
✚ Off map at d1 ✉ Caminho do Meio, Funchal ☎ 211 200 🕓 9–6 🚌 31 ♿ Few 🎫 Inexpensive (includes entrance to the nearby Jardim Botânico, ➤ 32)

JARDIM DE SANTA CATARINA

Younger children will enjoy the small playground and aviary in this public park. The park is dotted with sculptures and also has a little chapel.
✚ a3 ✉ Avenida do Infante, Funchal 🕓 24 hours 🍴 Café ♿ Few 🎫 Free

JEEP SAFARIS

Some of Madeira's more spectacular mountain roads are as yet unmetalled. While impassable to ordinary cars, they can be explored by jeep safari, which gives children the sense of being explorers of virgin territory. Safaris can be booked at travel agencies, or at Terras de Aventura, Caminho do Amparo 25 (☎ 776 818).

LEVADA WALKING

If you do not feel confident about *levada* walking with children on your own, let experienced guides show you the way. Various walks are on offer from Turismo Verde e Ecológico da Madeira (☎ 766 109). Other companies offering similar walks are Natura (☎ 236 015; www.madeirawalks.com) and Nature Meetings (☎ 200 618; www.naturemeetings.com).

LIDO COMPLEX

If your own hotel does not have an adequate pool, the municipal Lido Complex, in the Hotel Zone, has an Olympic-sized main pool, a children's pool, access to the sea from a diving platform and a choice of places to eat. It can be crowded at weekends, but less so during the week.
✉ Off map at a3 ✉ Rua do Gargulho 🕓 Apr–Sep: 8:30–7. Oct–Mar: 9–6

A yellow macaw, in the Jardim dos Loiros

Places to Swim

SWIMMING POOLS

Most of Madeira's beaches are very small and pebbly. Making up for the lack of sand, some hotels have magnificent pool complexes – led by the Savoy and the Crowne Plaza. If your hotel pool is too small, visit the public pools at the Lido (➤ 57) or the slightly more exclusive Clube Naval (➤ 81).

Splashing about in the children's pool of the Lido complex.

In the Top 25
20 PORTO SANTO (➤ 43)

CANIÇO
Non-residents can pay to use the pool and sea-bathing facilities at the Roca Mar Hotel, and the clear waters here are popular with divers. Local people come to swim off the rocky beach at Praia dos Reis Magos, a short walk to the east.
✚ E4 ✉ 8km east of Funchal

THE LIDO, FUNCHAL (➤ 57)

PONTA DELGADA
Across from the beachside church (➤ 55) is a rock-cut swimming pool, replenished by the tides and by Atlantic waves which dash against the walls showering bathers, much to the delight of children.
✚ C1 ✉ 51km north of Funchal 🚌 Bus 103 ♿ None

PORTO DO MONIZ
Bones weary from walking or jolting up and down the island's roads can be revived by a good soaking in the natural rock pools by the waterfront hotel. These have been enlarged to create a warm sea-water bathing area, just a few feet away from the Atlantic waves that crash against Madeira's northern shore.
✚ B1 ✉ 75km northwest of Funchal 🚌 80, 139 ♿ None

PRAINHA
Prainha has the largest natural sandy beach on Madeira, although it can be crowded in July and August. The beach is signposted along the road from Caniçal to Ponta de São Lourenço, and is reached down some steps beneath a chapel-topped hill. The brown-black sand on the beach derives from the local rock, a curious mixture of crushed shell and volcanic debris, pulverised by tens of thousands of years of wave action. The sheltered, south-facing beach enjoys good views of the easternmost tip of Madeira, as well as of aeroplanes flying into nearby Santa Catarina airport.
✚ F3 ✉ 30km east of Funchal 🚌 113 to Caniçal, then taxi ♿ Few

SANTA CRUZ (➤ 51)

SEIXAL
Here you can explore the rocky foreshore (follow the signs to Piscina for a group of big, sheltered rock pools) and walk along the jetty for views of the cliffs and waterfalls on either side of the tiny village.
✚ B2 ✉ 61km northwest of Funchal 🚌 80, 139 ♿ None

Places to Have Lunch

ARSÉNIO'S (££)
Come here to listen to *fado* music while you eat.
✉ Rua de Santa Maria 169, Funchal ☎ 224 007

BIO LOGOS (£)
Good fresh salads and vegetables are hard to find on Madeiran menus so eat healthily and help to keep this small wholefood and vegetarian restaurant in business.
✉ Rua Nova São Pedro, Funchal ☎ 236 868

CAFÉ DO TEATRO (£)
The most chic young Funchalese poseurs and artistic types come here, with the aim of being seen by their friends. Cool black and white décor and a pretty cobbled patio garden.
✉ Teatro Baltazar Dias, Avenida Arriaga, Funchal ☎ 236 400

CAFÉ ESPLENADA ARCO-VELHA (£)
Enjoy a simple but satisfying lunch of limpets and grilled sardines at this Old Town restaurant and watch the world go by from its pavement tables.
✉ Rua de Carlos I 42, Funchal

GOLDEN GATE (£)
Usually packed with Funchalese office workers, shoppers and people killing time before the bus home, this is the place where local people go for a snack.
✉ Avenida Arriaga 21, Funchal ☎ 220 053

HOTEL ESCOLA (££)
Five-star luxury service can be yours, even if you don't want to pay top prices. Madeira's Hotel School is where the island's aspiring chefs and waiters learn their skills. It offers a reasonably priced four-course menu, and a courtesy bus picks up guests from Funchal's Hotel Zone. Guests can use the pool, and there is afternoon tea from 4 to 6PM.
✉ Travessa dos Piornais, São Martinho ☎ 700 386

JARDIM DO CARREIRA (£)
Seek out the attractive courtyard garden at the rear of this bar for good inexpensive home cooking.
✉ Rua do Carreira 118, Funchal ☎ 222 498

JASMIN TEA HOUSE (£)
The lazy way to get to this house in the woods is to take a taxi or bus 47. Most visitors come here by walking from the Quinta do Palheiro gardens (the walk takes around 35 minutes).
✉ Quinta da Ribeira, Caminho dos Pretos 40, São Gonçalo
☎ 792 796

ON THE ROCKS

A good Madeiran any-time-of-day-snack is *lapas* – grilled limpets served in the shell, each in a puddle of garlic butter which you soak up with plenty of spongy homemade bread; in taste and texture limpets are very like snails.

Customers relax in the sun in an open-air café in Ribeira Brava

Attractions on Porto Santo

A smiling scuba diver, equipped for action in the waters off Porto Santo

---

In the Top 25

20 VILA BALEIRA (➤ 43)

FONTE DA AREIA

The little rain that Porto Santo receives rapidly filters through the island's sandy soils to emerge as a series of springs when the water meets impermeable basalt. The Fonte da Areia (Spring in the Sand) is one such spring, and its popularity is guaranteed by the belief that drinking its waters restores body and soul and bestows longevity. The spring can be reached on foot by taking the road west from Camacha.
✉ 3km northwest of Vila Baleira 🍴 Café (£) ♿ Few

PONTA DA CALHETA

This southernmost tip of Porto Santo marks the watershed between the long sweep of sandy beach running along the southern coast of the island and the rocky northern coast. A good time to come here is dusk, when the setting sun casts shadows and colours over the much-eroded rocks on the offshore islands. The evening can be extended by taking a meal of fresh fish in the nearby restaurant, then walking back along the sandy beach while imagining you are in your own private paradise.
✉ 5km southwest of Vila Baleira 🍴 Pôr-do-Sol (£££, ☎ 984 380) ♿ Few

PORTELA

The *miradouro* (viewpoint) at Portela may not be the highest point on Porto Santo, but it is the best place to get a sense of the scale of the pure sandy beach that seems to stretch endlessly along the southern coast. It will also give you an idea of why Porto Santo is known as the 'tawny island'. Deforestation at a very early stage in the island's history led to rapid erosion of the fertile topsoil, leaving the sand-coloured landscape you see today.
✉ 1.5km northeast of Vila Baleira ♿ Few

CASA MUSEU CRISTÓVÃO COLOMBO

This museum is housed in the building where Christopher Columbus reputedly lived during his stay on Porto Santo. There is a good library of books in English, Portuguese and other languages, from which you can learn all there is to know about the famous Genoese explorer. Several imaginative portraits and amusing prints depict the arrival of some of the first Europeans to land on American shores.
✉ Vila Baleira (in the street behind the parish church) ☎ 983 405
🕐 Tue–Fri 10–6; Sat, Sun, public hols 10–1

HOLY PEOPLE

The people of Porto Santo are known as *profetas,* because one of their number declared himself to be a messenger from God in the 16th century. Madeirans are known, in their turn, as *americanos,* because the people of Porto Santo consider them wealthy and flash.

MADEIRA
where to...

In Funchal

PRICES

Prices are approximate, based on a three-course meal for one, without drinks and service:

£ = under €15
££ = €15–€30
£££ = over €30

OPENING HOURS

Most restaurants in Funchal open from 11AM through to 11PM. Smarter restaurants close between 3 and 7.

A MURALHA (££)

As well as all the usual Madeiran specialities, A Muralha serves several more unusual regional dishes, including *picadinho* (fragrant herby stewed beef) and wild rabbit.
✉ Largo do Corpo Santo 2
☎ 232 561 🕐 Lunch, dinner

A RAMPA (££)

Located opposite the Savoy Hotel, A Rampa is popular with families and serves authentic pizzas and pasta dishes, including children's favourites such as macaroni and spaghetti Bolognese, as well as fresh salads and a range of more substantial fish and meat dishes, cooked Italian style. Friendly waiters and good-value prices.
✉ Henry II Building 1st Floor, Avenida do Infante ☎ 235 275
🕐 Lunch, dinner

ARSÉNIO'S (££)

Funchal's long-established *fado* house attracts mainland Portuguese holiday-makers and aficionados of the plaintive doom-laden songs of the Lisbon back streets. Listen while you eat.
✉ Rua de Santa Maria 169
☎ 224 007 🕐 Lunch, dinner

BAMBOO INN (££)

Good use is made of Madeira's unfailing supply of fresh fish and vegetables at this Chinese restaurant in the Hotel Zone – a good choice for when you cannot bear the idea of beef on a spit for dinner yet again.

✉ Estrada Monumental 318, 2nd Floor ☎ 766 861
🕐 Lunch, dinner

BIO LOGOS (£)

Tiny café specialising in vegetarian and organic food. No menu – just a range of good fresh salads, quiches, pies, casseroles and pizzas. The choice diminishes as the day goes on.
✉ Rua Nova São Pedro
☎ 236 868 🕐 Lunch only

BOMBAY PALACE (££)

This excellent tandoori restaurant makes a welcome change from a diet of Madeiran sardines, kebabs and tuna. Try the tandoori fish for an unusual starter.
✉ Eden Mar Shopping Centre, Rua do Gorgulho ☎ 763 110
🕐 Lunch, dinner

CASA CAROCHINHA (££)

Carochinha markets itself to English visitors as a home from home, with its lace tablecloths, bread-and-butter pudding and roast beef, but the restaurant also features many typically Madeiran dishes. Good-value set lunch menu.
✉ Rua de São Francesco 2
☎ 223 695 🕐 Lunch, dinner

CASA DOS REIS (££)

Intimate dining room decorated with topographical prints of Madeira; ideal for romantic candle-lit suppers. Charcoal-grilled lamb and fish specialities.
✉ Rua Impertriz Dona Amélia 101 ☎ 225 182
🕐 Lunch, dinner

CASA VELHA (£££)

Ceiling fans gently stir the air at this elegant restaurant – ideal for a special night out – set in a villa with flower-filled gardens. Specialises in flambé dishes and lobster.
✉ Rua Imperatriz Dona Amélia 69 ☎ 205 600 ⏰ Lunch, dinner

DOCA DO CAVACAS (££)

Not easily found (follow the road to the port and take the footpath beside the Duas Torres Hotel), this atmospheric restaurant enjoys magnificent sea views and specialises in fresh fish brought in by the fishing boats moored at the adjacent quay.
✉ Ponta da Cruz, Estrada Monumental ☎ 762 057 ⏰ Lunch, dinner

DON FILET (££)

Beef is king at this restaurant round the corner from the Savoy Hotel, where you can eat your fillets Brazilian style, broiled over a charcoal grill, or Madeiran style, skewered on a bay twig and flavoured with garlic.
✉ Rua do Favilo 7 ☎ 764 426 ⏰ Lunch, dinner. Closed Sun lunch

DONA AMÉLIA (££)

This elegant and well-restored town house with a terrace garden makes an atmospheric setting for the international-style cuisine served here.
✉ Rua Imperatriz Dona Amélia 83 ☎ 225 784 ⏰ Lunch, dinner

LES FAUNES (£££)

Arguably Madeira's best restaurant, and the place to eat if expense is no object. It serves top-quality international cuisine in a bright and airy dining room, decorated with Picasso drawings of fauns. Impeccable service. Though not as formal as Reid's Dining Room (➤ 72), you need to dress smartly. Reservations advised.
✉ Reid's Hotel, Estrada Monumental ☎ 717 171 ⏰ Lunch, dinner

FLEUR DE LYS (£££)

For not much more than the cost of a meal in some of Funchal's downtown restaurants, you can savour the sophistication of the Savoy Hotel's flagship restaurant, while enjoying panoramic views over Funchal and the harbour. Reservations essential.
✉ Savoy Hotel, Avenida do Infante ☎ 222 031 ⏰ Lunch, dinner

GAVIÃO NOVO (££)

This smart restaurant in the Old Town specialises in fish. It is always worth asking the waiters what is best because they often have specials not listed on the main menu – it all depends what the fishermen have managed to hook.
✉ Rua Santa Maria 131 ☎ 229 238 ⏰ Lunch, dinner

HONG KONG (££)

Authentic Cantonese-style food.
✉ Olimpo Shopping Centre, Avenida do Infante ☎ 228 181 ⏰ Lunch, dinner

TAKING A TAXI

If you take a taxi to a restaurant, be prepared for the taxi driver to try to persuade you to try a different establishment; they may tell you that they know a better and cheaper restaurant, very special and known only to locals. Take their advice if you wish, but be aware that the taxi driver is probably getting commission from the restaurant, that it will often be out of town (hence the taxi driver earns a bigger fare for taking you there) and that if you do not like the restaurant or its prices there will probably not be a cheaper alternative in the neighbourhood.

In Funchal

GARLIC BREAD

When you sit down to eat in a Madeiran restaurant the waiter will probably present you with a basket of homemade bread, spread with garlic butter and warmed in the oven – a delicious accompaniment to pre-dinner drinks while you contemplate the menu.

FISH ON THE MENU

Your favourite fish may not seem so familiar if the menu lists them in Portuguese only. Here is a short list of names that you will frequently find on Madeiran menus: *atum* is tuna; *bacalhau* is salted cod; *cherne* is sea bass; *carapau* is mackerel; *pargo* is bream; *salmão* is salmon; *salmonete* is red mullet; *truta* is trout; *espadarte* is swordfish (not to be confused with *espada*, the ubiquitous Madeiran speciality scabbard fish).

LE JARDIN (££)

French influences are to be found in the cooking at this Old Town restaurant specialising in flambé fish and peppered steak.
✉ Rua de Carlos I 60 ☎ 222 864 🕓 Lunch, dinner

KON TIKI (££)

After a week of meat kebabs and *espada* (scabbard fish), visitors seeking a change could do worse than visit Kon Tiki for beef broiled on hot lava stones (Finnish style) or shark steak. Inevitably, *espada* is on offer too, but here the flamboyant waiters flambé the fish at your table with prawns.
✉ Rua do Favila 9 ☎ 764 737 🕓 Lunch, dinner

LONDRES (££)

Despite the name, Londres specialises in mainland Portuguese dishes, including *bacalhau* (salt cod) for which there are said to be as many recipes as there are days in the year. Here they serve a different Portuguese speciality every day.
✉ Rua da Carreira 64A ☎ 235 329 🕓 Lunch, dinner. Closed Sun

MAR AZUL (££)

Do not be put off by the sight of waiters outside touting for business. The food is excellent, as is the entertainment – Madeiran folk dancers perform authentic island dances on the pavement outside and even those who hate the idea of 'folk' will be charmed. Prices are reasonable so long as you avoid the lobster.
✉ Funchal Yacht Marina, Avenida das Comunidades Madeirenses ☎ 230 079 🕓 Lunch, dinner

MARINA TERRACE (££)

Another waterside restaurant on the northern rim of the Yacht Marina, serving everything from pizza to lobster. Staff are in Madeiran costume and there is folk dancing on Monday and Saturday nights and *fado* music on Tuesdays, Thursdays and Sundays, from around 7:30.
✉ Marina do Funchal ☎ 230 547 🕓 Lunch, dinner

MARISA (££)

When you visit this tiny Old Town restaurant you feel as if you are a guest in someone's home, as father and son cook delicious seafood and rice dishes while mother takes the orders and waits at table. Very good value.
✉ Rua de Santa Maria 162 ☎ 226 189 🕓 Lunch, dinner

MOBY DICK (££)

Fish restaurant in the Hotel Zone serving a wide range of fresh fish, from *espada de camarão* (scabbard fish with prawns) to *atum con todos* (tuna with everything!).
✉ Estrada Monumental 187 ☎ 776 868 🕓 Lunch, dinner

O ALMIRANTE (££)

Walls decorated with nautical memorabilia set the theme for this popular Old Town restaurant specialising in meat on the spit, fish and shellfish.
✉ Largo do Poço 1–2 ☎ 224 252 🕓 Lunch, dinner

O CELEIRO (££)

The Cellar is a good place to sample *caldeirada* (fish casserole).

Rua dos Aranhas 22
230 622 Lunch, dinner

O JANGO (££)

This intimate Old Town restaurant, converted from a former fisherman's home, specialises in seafood.

Rua de Santa Maria 166
221 280 Lunch, dinner.
Closed 1–21 Jul

O PANORÂMICO (£££)

If you like music with your meal, this is the place to come. The flagship restaurant at the Pestana Carlton Park Hotel offers dinner dances and live entertainment every Wednesday and Saturday.

Pestana Carlton Park Hotel, Rua Imperatriz Dona Amélia
209 100 Dinner

O TAPASSOL (££)

A favourite of old Madeira hands, this Old Town restaurant has a tiny roof-top terrace for outdoor dining and a menu featuring less-usual dishes, such as wild rabbit in season and octopus casserole.

Rua Dom Carlos I 62
225 023 Lunch, dinner

PORTÃO (££)

Portão is a quieter and more intimate restaurant than those on the main drag. Save space for delicious Zabaglione Madeira, the classic Italian dessert made with Madeira rather than Marsala.

Rua Portão de São Tiago 1
221 125 Lunch, dinner

PRINCE ALBERT (££)

Themed as a Victorian pub, the Prince Albert tends to attract a mainly British crowd. It serves good Portuguese and international food.

Rua Imperatriz Dona Amélia 86 235 793 Lunch, dinner

QUINTA PALMEIRA (£££)

This 19th-century *quinta* is a rare survivor of the mansions that lined Avenida do Infante before the high-rise hotel blocks arrived. Eat in the elegant, mirrored dining room, or on the garden terrace.

Avenida do Infante 5
221 814 Lunch, dinner

SALSA LATINA (££)

Popular late-night haunt (open until 2AM) with a cocktail bar, terrace restaurant and live Brazilian-style music.

Rua Imperatriz Dona Amélia 101 225 182 Lunch, dinner (high season only)

VAGRANT (££)

Children will enjoy the novelty of eating on board ship in this 'floating' restaurant on the Funchal waterfront (but there is little risk of seasickness – this restaurant is now firmly bedded in concrete). The tall-masted schooner was formerly owned by the Beatles, hence it is often referred to as the 'Beatles' Boat'. The menu ranges from pizzas and ice cream to typical Madeiran dishes.

Avenida das Comunidades Madeirenses 223 572
Lunch, dinner

ACCOMPANIMENTS

Any dish you order on Madeira is likely to be served with seasonal vegetables and salad. Chips are nearly always served as an accompaniment to meat dishes, and boiled potatoes with fish, unless you request otherwise. Banana fried in butter is an unusual but tasty accompaniment to many fish dishes, as is maize meal, formed into cubes and fired until the outside is crisp.

FOR A TREAT

On special occasions Madeirans eat kebabs – called *espetada* – made from cubes of prime beef, rubbed in sea salt and minced garlic and skewered on a fresh bay twig. To enjoy this dish at its most authentic, you have to eat it at a village festival, or find a restaurant that grills the meat over a wood fire for extra fragrance.

Around the Island

MADEIRAN WINE

As well as fortified Madeira wine, the island's vineyards produce a range of local red wines, which are drunk young, while they are still fresh, fruity and relatively low in alcohol. You may not find Madeiran wines on the wine list – restaurateurs prefer to sell more expensive imported wines with a higher mark-up – but you can try asking for local wine in snack bars and cafés.

WHERE DO YOU START?

Purists might argue that the best way to sample the four different types of Madeira is to work steadily through the repertoire, starting with dry *sercial* as an aperitif, then moving on to medium-dry *verdelho* with the main course, and nutty *bual* with dessert, reserving the rich, dark *malmsey* to drink with coffee.

However, few Madeirans would drink fortified Madeira wine with their food, preferring something lighter.

BOCA DA ENCUMEADA

ENCUMEADA RESTAURANT (££)

This roadside restaurant specialises in the kind of food that is rarely found elsewhere on the island – rabbit, suckling pig and hearty mountain beef and vegetable casseroles.

✉ 2km south of Boca da Encumeada ☎ 952 319 🕓 Lunch, dinner 🚌 6, 139

CAMACHA

A CORNÉLIA (£)

A simple restaurant serving good home cooking at reasonable prices.

✉ Vale do Paraiso, just south of Camacha ☎ 792 892 🕓 Lunch, dinner 🚌 29, 77

CANIÇO

INN AND ART (££)

This friendly cliff-top establishment in Caniço de Baixa combines a restaurant, wine bar, café and hotel with a gallery of original paintings by contemporary artists from all over the world, many of which are for sale. Good range of wines.

✉ Caniço de Baixo R61/R62 ☎ 938 200 🕓 Lunch, dinner 🚌 2, 113, 114, 155

LA PERLA GOURMET RESTAURANT (£££)

Set in beautifully gardened grounds, La Perla occupies a typical Madeiran *quinta*, a manor house once at the centre of a wine estate, now converted to provide a stylish restaurant. The Italian-influenced menu includes wild mushroom dishes, veal and zabaglione, as well as grilled fish and, in tribute to Madeira's volcanic origins, beef served sizzling on a heated volcanic stone.

✉ Quinta Splendida, Sitio da Vargem ☎ 930 400 🕓 Lunch, dinner 🚌 2, 113, 114, 155

LA TERRAÇA (££)

This restaurant with its outdoor terrace setting is ideal for long lazy lunches, or dinner in the balmy evening air, while enjoying the valley views down to the sea. Fish is the speciality.

✉ Sitio da Vargem ☎ 933 898 🕓 Lunch, dinner 🚌 2, 113, 114, 155

VILLAGE PUB (£)

This English-run bar and restaurant is popular for its true pub atmosphere. The speciality is Full English Breakfast (served throughout opening hours). There is a good choice of beers, and bar snacks are available.

✉ Town centre ☎ 932 596 🕓 Noon–2AM. Closed Mon 🚌 2, 113, 114, 155

GARAJAU

VISTA MAR (££)

You can sample typical Portuguese cuisine, with different daily specials, at this popular seafront restaurant, five minutes' walk from the Dom Pedro Hotel in Garajau.

✉ Seafront ☎ 934 110 🕓 Lunch, dinner 🚌 2, 113, 114, 155

MACHICO

MERCADO VELHO (££)

Machico's Old Market makes an atmospheric base for this pleasant restaurant with its tree-shaded terrace and fountain.

✉ Rua do Mercado ☎ 965 926 ⏱ Lunch, dinner 🚌 20, 23, 53, 78, 113, 156

O FACHO (££)

A lively restaurant which is popular with locals. The snack bar is ideal for simple eats, or for a more formal occasion, try the dining room next door.

✉ Praça do Salazar ☎ 962 786 ⏱ Lunch, dinner 🚌 20, 23, 53, 78, 113, 156

PASTELARIA GALÃ (£)

Pop in here for afternoon tea and sample the delights of Madeiran cakes, made with eggs, almonds, fruits and nuts. The restaurant also serves snacks and sandwiches.

✉ Rua da Mercado ☎ 965 720 ⏱ Lunch, dinner 🚌 20, 23, 53, 78, 113, 156

MONTE

ALDEIA DO MONTE (££)

The Aldeia do Monte commands sweeping views over Funchal and the harbour from its position in Monte village. The restaurant features German, Portuguese and international dishes, with tables on the terrace for informal snacks and a rustic dining room inside.

✉ Sítio do Pico ☎ 783 547 ⏱ Lunch, dinner 🚌 Town bus 20, 21. Rural bus 103, 138

PICO DO ARIEIRO

POUSADA DO PICO DO ARIEIRO (££)

The *pousada* (government-run hotel) on top of Madeira's third-highest peak caters for hungry walkers in the café, with traditional Madeira fare, while the upmarket restaurant serves international-style food and offers fine views.

✉ Pico do Arieiro ☎ 230 110 ⏱ Lunch, dinner

POISO

CASA DE ABRIGO (££)

Sitting in woodland in the middle of the countryside, this roadside restaurant draws its trade from hungry walkers exploring the mountainous centre of the island. The welcoming old-fashioned interior is warmed by a wood fire (at this altitude the air has a chill even in summer) which is also used for cooking the traditional Madeiran meat-on-a-spit.

✉ At the crossroads ☎ 782 269 ⏱ Lunch, dinner 🚌 103, 132, 138

PORTO DO MONIZ

CACHALOTE (££)

Enjoy fine views of the waves breaking against the rocky foreshore of Madeira's northern coast. The locally caught fish and seafood served here is as fresh as it can be.

✉ On the seafront ☎ 853 180 ⏱ Lunch, dinner. Closed Oct–Mar 🚌 8, 139, 150

A FEAST OF FRUIT

Fruit lovers will be spoiled for choice on Madeira, where tropical bananas, mangos, avocados, guavas, passion fruits, papaws, prickly pears and custard apples thrive on the sunny southern coastal strip, and the cooler mountain orchards produce cherries, pears, strawberries, walnuts and small but intensely flavoured apples. Because of Madeira's equitable climate, many of these fruits are in season all year round.

SEAFOOD AND SOUPS

Many restaurants on Madeira specialise in seafood, though most is imported and a seafood platter can be expensive. Fish soup is, by contrast, delicious and cheap, being based on stock made from the heads and bones of locally caught fish, such as sea-bream, black-tail, barracuda and tuna.

Around the Island

MADEIRAN DESSERTS

Although Madeirans have a sweet tooth, they do not normally eat puddings – desserts in most restaurants will be limited to a choice between fruit and several kinds of ice cream. When they want to indulge, Madeirans go to a *pastelaria*, a baker specialising in sweet pastries, most of which are based on nuts, dried fruit or egg custard. *Bolo de mel* is a dark molasses-rich cake, sold all over Madeira, made from almonds and dried fruits seasoned with cloves, aniseed and fruit peel. Also delicious is *queijadas da Madeira* (Madeiran cheesecake).

FERNANDES (£)

Close to the Cachalote, this seasonal seafood restaurant is cheap, clean and friendly, which is why Portuguese holiday-makers flock here during the summer months.
✉ On north side of main square ☎ 853 147 ⏰ Lunch, dinner. Closed Oct–Mar 🚌 8, 139, 150

ORCA (££)

The fact that many coach parties stop off here for lunch should not be taken as a sign that the food is inferior tourist fare. On the contrary, everything is fresh and well presented and the portions are large. Good views over the rock pools of Porto Moniz.
✉ On south side of main square ☎ 850 000 ⏰ Lunch, dinner 🚌 8, 139, 150

POLO NORTE (£)

The North Pole has a snack bar as well as a formal dining room, and is therefore a good choice if you just want a light meal or your children are hungry for a burger.
✉ On north side of main square ☎ 853 322 ⏰ Lunch, dinner 🚌 8, 139, 150

QUINTA DO PALHEIRO

CASA VELHA DO PALHEIRO (£££)

Outside of Funchal's five-star hotels, it is unusual to find cooking of gourmet-standard on Madeira. This elegant restaurant, in a converted mansion on the edge of the Quinta do Palheiro estate, is a rare exception: the stylish dishes served here combine the best of Madeira's fresh ingredients with ideas borrowed from Italy, the Mediterranean and the Far East.
✉ Estalagem Casa Velha do Palheiro ☎ 794 901 ⏰ Lunch, dinner. Booking advised 🚌 Town buses 29, 36, 37

RIBEIRA BRAVA

ÁGUA MAR (£)

With a terrace for fair-weather dining and a glassed-in dining room for when the sea spray gets rough, this inexpensive restaurant serves standard Madeiran fare.
✉ On the seafront ☎ 951 148 ⏰ Lunch, dinner. Closed Oct–Mar 🚌 4, 6, 7, 80, 107, 115, 127, 139, 142

RIBEIRO FRIO

VICTOR'S BAR (££)

This popular roadside restaurant serves fresh trout from the adjacent trout farm.
✉ Main street ☎ 575 898 ⏰ Lunch, dinner 🚌 103, 138

SÃO JORGE

AS CABANAS (££)

This restaurant, hotel and shopping complex, set down in the countryside between São Jorge and Arco de São Jorge, has African-style circular huts for rooms and a circular dining room. Keen prices and excellent Madeiran food make this a popular stopping-off point.
✉ Sítio da Beira da Quinta ☎ 576 291 ⏰ Lunch, dinner 🚌 103, 132, 138

SÃO VICENTE

O VIRGÍLIO (£)

O Virgílio looks like a tourist trap, but it retains the atmosphere of a good-value village bar, serving everything from a sandwich to kebabs cooked over the log fire.

✉ On Porto Moniz road ☎ 842 467 🕐 Lunch, dinner 🚌 6, 132, 139, 150

QUEBRA MAR (££)

The Quebra Mar serves standard Madeiran fare of kebabs and scabbard fish, plus grilled meats and fish.

✉ On the seafront ☎ 842 338 🕐 Lunch, dinner 🚌 6, 132, 139, 150

SÃO MARTINHO

BODIÃO (££)

Dine out on the slopes of Pico dos Barcelos, the volcanic peak just north of Funchal's Hotel Zone, where the views, on a clear day, are wonderful.

✉ Caminho de São Martinho ☎ 263 078 🕐 Lunch, dinner 🚌 4, 6, 107, 154

SANTANA

O COLMO (££)

Santana's main restaurant attracts large tour groups, but the food is excellent.

✉ Main street ☎ 573 666 🕐 Lunch, dinner 🚌 103, 132, 138

QUINTA DO FURÃO (££)

This is a working wine estate where visitors are encouraged to explore the vineyards, sample locally produced wines and eat in the snack bar or the more upmarket restaurant.

✉ Achada do Gramacho ☎ 570 100 🕐 Lunch, dinner 🚌 103, 132, 138

PORTO SANTO

BAR TORRES (£)

Roast chicken as you probably haven't tasted it for a long time draws appreciative crowds to this bar with its vine-covered dining terrace; on the road to Fonte da Areia.

✉ Camacha ☎ 984 373 🕐 Lunch, dinner; booking essential in high season

MAR E SOL (££)

This deservedly popular restaurant sits near Porto Santo's glorious beach, midway between Vila Baleira and Ponta da Calheta. It serves fresh fish and seafood.

✉ Campo de Baixo ☎ 982 269 🕐 Lunch, dinner

O FORNO (££)

A variation on the usual theme of *espetada* kebabs is the house speciality, *picado*, consisting of small chunks of beef spiced up with garlic and chilli. The excellent home-baked bread is cooked in the wood-fired oven that gives the restaurant its name.

✉ Rampa da Fontinha, Vila Baleira ☎ 985 141 🕐 Lunch, dinner

PÔR-DO-SOL (£££)

This smart daytime café and night-time restaurant serves wonderful grilled fish but is best known for its views of the setting sun from Porto Santo's southernmost tip.

✉ Calheta ☎ 984 380 🕐 Lunch, dinner

LIQUEURS

Madeirans have a gift for turning even the most unlikely ingredients into alcoholic liqueurs. As you tour the island you will be offered local specialities, such as the delicious *ginga*, made from cherries, *castanha*, produced from sweet chestnuts, and *maracujá*, made from passion fruit. Liqueurs are also made from fennel (*funcho*), almonds (*amêndo*), walnuts (*noz*) and banana (*banau*). Less palatable to many, but a powerful cold remedy, is the menthol-flavoured *eucolipto* liqueur made from the seeds of the island's ubiquitous eucalyptus trees.

Popular as a pick-me-up is *poncha*, a cocktail of sugar-cane spirit, called *aguardente*, mixed with honey and fresh lemon juice.

In Funchal

PRICES

Prices are for a double room, excluding breakfast and tax:

£ = under €50
££ = €50–€100
£££ = over €100

The prices for rooms in the more expensive hotels are often cheaper if booked as part of a package holiday. Conversely, the tour companies often charge more for the cheaper hotels than you could get by booking direct. Nearly all hotels in Madeira include breakfast as part of the room price. Half- and full-board terms are available at the more expensive hotels.

CASTANHEIRO APARTAMENTOS (££)

This apartment hotel offers bright, well-furnished rooms, with air-conditioning, TV and CD player, plus a kitchenette and dining area, in the heart of Funchal. The hotel is opposite the University of Madeira, just north of the Praça do Município – during the day the street bustles with students, but there is little traffic after dark. Facilities include a restaurant, snack bar and private parking.
✉ Rua do Castanheiro 27 ☎ 227 060 ⏰ All year

CLIFF BAY (£££)

The Cliff Bay Resort Hotel is just around the corner from Reid's and enjoys similar panoramic views of Funchal and the harbour. It has rooms designed especially for visitors with disabilities and there is a large outdoor pool, an indoor heated pool, health club, tennis and squash courts, gym and sauna.
✉ Estrada Monumental 147 ☎ 707 700; www.portobay.com ⏰ All year

D'AJUDA (££)

This hotel and apartment complex, 3.5km from the centre of Funchal, is ideal for people who want to combine the freedom of self-catering with the facilities of a four-star hotel. Choose between twin-bedded hotel rooms with balconies, studio apartments for 2–3 people with kitchenettes, or 4-bed apartments. Facilities include outdoor and indoor pools, and a free minibus service to Funchal.
✉ Caminho Velha da Ajuda, São Martinho ☎ 761 316 ⏰ All year

EDEN MAR (££)

Excellent-value aparthotel close to the supermarkets and the Lido complex in the Hotel Zone. The studios and suites all have a kitchenette. The site has a pool, gym, sauna, jacuzzi and tennis courts.
✉ Rua do Gorgulho 2 ☎ 709 700; www.portobay.com ⏰ All year

ESTRELICIA (££)

The Estrelicia forms part of a complex with two other hotels, in a quiet area of the Hotel Zone, sharing heated swimming pools, tennis courts, restaurants and a gym. There is a regular minibus service into Funchal. In the same complex is the Mimosa Aparthotel (☎ 765 021), whose rooms have sink, fridge and cooking rings for self-catering. The complex has an active entertainments programme.
✉ Caminho Velha do Ajuda ☎ 706 600 ⏰ All year

MADEIRA (££)

This small hotel looking out over the Jardim de São Francisco public gardens could not be more central, but being one block back from Funchal's main street, it remains a peaceful spot. Comfortably furnished rooms, friendly service and a small roof-top pool.
✉ Rua Ivens 21 ☎ 230 071 ⏰ All year

MADEIRA PALÁCIO (£££)

Being 5km from the city centre, the Madeira Palácio is less expensive than rival five-star hotels, and is a good choice if you want luxury in peaceful surroundings at bargain prices. Instead of views over Funchal, rooms look towards the towering cliffs of Cabo Girão. A courtesy bus provides a regular service into Funchal, but many visitors prefer to stay in the hotel, enjoying the pool, gardens, tennis courts, games room and sauna, plus nightly live music and regular folklore evenings.

✉ Estrada Monumental 265
☎ 702 702 ⏰ All year

MONTE CARLO (££)

The steep walk up to this hotel is rewarded by the views to be had across the red-tiled roofs of Funchal from the terrace and from many rooms. The oldest part of the hotel consists of an elegant 19th-century mansion, and the modern rooms are built in traditional Madeiran style. Facilities include a restaurant, bar and a mini-bus service into town.

✉ Calçada da Saúde 10
☎ 226 131 ⏰ All year

PESTANA CARLTON MADEIRA (£££)

Along with the Savoy and the Pestana Carlton Park, the Carlton Madeira enjoys a location close to downtown Funchal. The hotel is in two parts; rooms in the 16-storey main block enjoy fine views to the harbour or to the mountains, while the pool terrace block has rooms looking over the hotel's two large swimming pools. Other facilities include a paddling pool, tennis courts, mini golf, a gym and a sauna. For children, there is a play area, and a kids' activity club (during the summer).

✉ Largo António Nobre
☎ 239 500; www.pestana.com
⏰ All year

PESTANA CARLTON PARK HOTEL (£££)

The Pestana Carlton Park is the closest of Madeira's five-star hotels to the centre of Funchal; from here it is a short stroll through the Jardim de Santa Catarina to the downtown area. This is also Madeira's liveliest hotel for nightlife, with a top-class cabaret programme (➤ 82), regular discos and a casino on the grounds. The architecture was adventurous in its day: designed in the 1970s by Oscar Niemeyer, the Brazilian architect, the hotel follows Corbusian principles in being built on stilts to allow uninterrupted views across the hotel gardens to the sea. The circular casino in the grounds is known locally (and perhaps disparagingly) as the 'rack of lamb'. Rooms are large and well equipped and there are good swimming and tennis facilities in the grounds.

✉ Rua Imperatriz Dona Amélia
☎ 209 100; www.pestana.com
⏰ All year

A ROOM WITH A VIEW

Hotels charge up to 20 per cent extra for a room with a sea view. You may consider this worth while if the alternative is a room on the street side of the hotel, for many rooms in the Hotel Zone look out on the busy Estrada Monumental. Before booking your hotel, you may also wish to check whether there is any noisy construction work underway nearby, especially if you are planning to stay in the Hotel Zone.

In Funchal

LOCATION, LOCATION

Hotels on Madeira tend to be priced according to location: the closer to the city centre, the higher the price. To be really central, opt for the Savoy or Pestana Carlton Park. Reid's is, despite its luxurious ambiance, some 30 minutes' walk from the centre, and most of the hotels in the Hotel Zone are farther out still. Those some way from the town centre are often the cheapest, however, and they represent a good bargain since many provide a courtesy bus into town.

SELF-CATERING

For visitors with families, the option of self-catering may appeal if you want to make your own meals for the children. Ask your travel agent about the availability of aparthotels, where the accommodation includes a small kitchen and a living room.

PORTO SANTA MARIA (£££)

This new hotel in the Zona Velha brings four-star luxury to a part of Funchal that has only had cheap and old-fashioned accommodation up to now. The hotel is perfectly located for visitors who want to be right where the action is, without sacrificing the facilities of an upmarket hotel. It is fronted by a sun terrace with outdoor pool and bar, and some of Funchal's best restaurants are literally on the doorstep.
✉ Avenida do Mar ☎ 206 700; www.portobay.com ⏱ All year

QUINTA DA BELA VISTA (££)

You need a car to reach this elegant mansion hotel (some 15 minutes from the centre) but the price is worth paying for stylishly furnished rooms, many with antiques, and polished service.
✉ Caminho Avista Navios 4 ☎ 706 400 ⏱ All year

QUINTA DA PENHA DE FRANÇA (££)

Many *quintas* (aristocratic mansions) were swept away when the Hotel Zone was created in the 1980s, but this fine building managed to survive in a prime spot behind the Pestana Carlton Park Hotel. Now converted to a hotel itself, the Quinta is a place of old-fashioned elegance combined with all mod cons.
✉ Rua Penha de França 2 ☎ 204 650 ⏱ All year

QUINTA DO SOL (££)

This friendly hotel overlooks the gardens of the Quinta do Magnólia park, with its tennis and squash courts, which guests can use for a small charge. The hotel also has its own heated swimming pool and games room. For an added touch of luxury, go for rooms in the new wing. The hotel puts on a weekly folklore show, plus live music most nights.
✉ Rua Dr Pita 6 ☎ 764 151 ⏱ All year

QUINTA PERESTRELO (££)

This small 19th-century mansion has rooms overlooking the public gardens of the nearby Quinta do Magnólia. Friendly service.
✉ Rua do Dr Pita 3 ☎ 763 720 ⏱ All year

REID'S PALACE (£££)

Reid's is one of the world's best-known prestigious hotels, gaining its name for quiet sophistication in the days when the rich and leisured classes would spend the winter on Madeira to escape the cold of northern Europe. William Reid, the founder, one of 12 sons of an impoverished Scottish crofter, worked his passage to Madeira in 1836 and set up a rental agency. Wealthy visitors would rely on Reid to find them a villa for their stay, paying him handsomely to do so. With the money he made, he bought the cliff-top site of Reid's Hotel, with its uninterrupted sea views and immaculate gardens.

Reid died in 1888 before seeing his dream hotel completed: it opened in 1891, and has numbered royalty, film stars and heads of state among its guests. For some, this elegant, understated hotel will be far too formal (most guests wear evening dress for dinner); for others it will be a welcome escape from the bustling world.

✉ Estrada Monumental 139
☎ 717 171; www.reidspalace.com ⚙ All year

RESIDENCIAL GORDON (£)

The Gordon is a quiet, old-fashioned hotel, furnished in a style that remains popular on Madeira but which went out of fashion elsewhere in the 1950s. Some rooms overlook the gardens of the English Church.

✉ Rua do Quebra Costas 34
☎ 742 366 ⚙ All year

RESIDENCIAL SANTA CLARA (£)

This hotel offers budget accommodation in a dignified old building with grand interiors; the catch is that it is a stiff uphill walk from the centre of Funchal, past the Santa Clara Convent, so you need to be fit to get here.

✉ Calçada do Pico 16B ☎ 742 194 ⚙ All year

SAVOY (£££)

One of Madeira's longest-established luxury hotels, the Savoy is quiet and dignified but caters well for families, with friendly staff and excellent sports facilities. Swimmers have a choice of four pools, including the luxurious facilities of the tropical lido. There are also tennis courts, a games room and a health centre, plus a library for those who prefer less strenuous activities. Rooms are large and the hotel is a 15-minute stroll from downtown Funchal.

✉ Avenida do Infante
☎ 222 031 ⚙ All year

SIRIUS (£)

Comfortable rooms at reasonable prices in a bustling street in the heart of Funchal.

✉ Rua das Hortas 31–37
☎ 226 117 ⚙ All year

VILA RAMOS (££)

Enjoy the facilities of the Savoy Hotel without paying luxury hotel prices. The Vila Ramos is under the same management as the Savoy, and guests can use that hotel's facilities. The hotel is in a quiet location, 15 minutes from the shops and restaurants of the Lido area, and with a regular mini-bus service to downtown Funchal. Rooms are larger than average, with balconies.

✉ Azinhaga da Casa Branca 7
☎ 706 280 ⚙ All year

WINDSOR (£)

This friendly modern hotel is in the maze of lanes near the Carmo church in central Funchal. Most rooms face into an inner courtyard. There is parking and a tiny roof-top pool.

✉ Rua das Hortas 4C
☎ 233081 ⚙ All year

HIGH AND LOW SEASON

Hotel prices on Madeira reflect the demand at different times of the year. Late July and all of August is expensive because Portuguese holiday-makers come to the island to escape the heat of the mainland. The two weeks of Christmas and New Year cost even more because many people come for the illuminations and the spectacular New Year fireworks: hotels not only charge extra at this time of year, they also add in the cost of compulsory dinner dance tickets for Christmas Eve, Christmas Day and New Year's Eve. By contrast, January, February, March and November are low season months, when some real bargains can be had, even at such prestigious hotels as Reid's.

Around Madeira and Porto Santo

QUINTAS, ESTALAGEMS AND RESIDENCIALS

Rural hotels on Madeira go by a variety of different names, but usually any establishment that calls itself an *estalagem* or a *residencial* is a small hotel, with perhaps 30 or so rooms, that prides itself on a certain character. Many are conversions of rural mansions, as are *quintas* – *quinta* being the Portuguese word for a manor house at the centre of a wine or agricultural estate.

CALHETA

JARDIM DO ATLANTICO (£££)

One of the few luxury hotels in western Madeira, the Jardim do Atlantico promotes itself as a health resort. Yoga, meditation, massage, hydrotherapy and acupuncture are available, as well as fitness classes and countryside walks. The restaurant also offers vegetarian dishes.

✉ Lomba da Rocha, Prazeres, ☎ 822 200 🕐 All year

CAMACHA

ESTALAGEM RELÓGIO (£)

Some of the good-value rooms in this *estalagem* have spectacular views. The nearby restaurant has Madeiran song and dance shows by one of the island's best troupes.

✉ Sítio da Igreja ☎ 922 777 🕐 All year

CANIÇO

QUINTA SPLENDIDA (£££)

The pink-walled *quinta* now houses the excellent restaurant; the modern guest rooms are set around a courtyard, surrounded by tropical gardens.

✉ Sítio de Vargem ☎ 930 400 🕐 All year

ROCA MAR (£££)

The Roca Mar enjoys a spectacular location on the cliff tops south of Caniço. The rocky cove at the foot of the cliffs has been converted into a lido. The hotel has a diving club, plus evening entertainment and a shuttle bus to Funchal.

✉ Caniço de Baixa ☎ 934 334 🕐 All year

ROYAL ORCHID (££)

This aparthotel complex, alongside the Roca Mar, has indoor and outdoor pools, a jacuzzi, a Turkish steam room and sauna, gym and games rooms. The apartments are built in terraced blocks with sea views; each studio has its own kitchenette.

✉ Caniço de Baixo ☎ 934 600 🕐 All year

MACHICO

RESIDENCIAL MACHICO (£)

In the heart of town and a good choice for budget travellers, with private bathrooms and plenty of restaurants nearby.

✉ Praça Salazar ☎ 965 575 🕐 All year

PICO DO ARIEIRO

POUSADA DO PICO DO ARIEIRO (££)

Perched high above the clouds, on top of Pico do Arieiro, 1,818m above sea level, this state-run hotel enjoys stunning views of the volcanic landscapes of Madeira's central mountain range. Visitors come here to get an early start on their hiking trips to Pico Ruivo, or to watch the spectacular effects created by the rising and setting sun, or to enjoy the clarity and detail of the night sky.

✉ Pico do Arieiro ☎ 230 110 🕐 All year; book well in advance

PORTO DO MONIZ

RESIDENCIAL ORCA (££)

This small 12-room hotel is perched above the rock pools on Madeira's north-westernmost tip. Thanks to its popularity with round-the-island travellers, the village is now a surprisingly busy and cosmopolitan spot.

✉ Sitio das Poças
☎ 850 000 🕐 All year

SÃO JORGE

CABANAS DE SÃO JORGE (££)

Guests stay in round huts inspired by Zulu architecture (the owner spent many years in South Africa), set among pine and eucalyptus trees. There are fine views from the carefully tended gardens over the cliffs of Madeira's north coast.

✉ Sitio da Beira da Quinta
☎ 576 291; cabanasvillage.com
🕐 All year

SÃO VICENTE

ESTALAGEM DO MAR (££)

Built in a crescent shape on the edge of the sea, the modern Estalagem do Mar has rooms that look out over the circular outdoor pool to the rocky foreshore. Facilities include an indoor heated pool, a games room, a sauna and a gym.

✉ Sao Viçente
☎ 840 010
🕐 All year

SERRA DA ÁGUA

ESTALAGEM DO SANTO (££)

Popular with golfers, the Estalagem do Santo is a short drive from the Santo da Serra golf course. Set among woodland, with manicured grounds and a new indoor swimming pool, the hotel has modern rooms built around the core of a 200-year-old mansion.

✉ Santo António da Serra
☎ 552 595 🕐 All year

POUSADA DOS VINHÁTICOS (££)

This charming *pousada* caters for walkers exploring the unspoiled woodland terrain in the spectacular Serra da Água Valley, south of the Encumeada pass. Facilities are simple but adequate.

✉ Serra da Água ☎ 952 344
🕐 All year; book in advance

PORTO SANTO

LUAMAR (££)

Among the sand dunes; rooms have kitchenettes and there is a small supermarket on site. A shuttle bus runs to Vila Baleira.

✉ Sítio de Cabeço de Ponta
☎ 984 121 🕐 May–Oct only

PORTO SANTO (£££)

The beautiful gardens of this hotel merge with Porto Santo's golden beach. Windsurfing boards and bicycles are available, plus a mini golf course and tennis courts.

✉ Ribeiro Cochino, Campo de Baixo ☎ 982 381 🕐 May–Oct only

POUSADAS

Pousadas are a unique Portuguese institution – a chain of state-run inns set in scenic locations, often in important historic buildings. The two on Madeira are relatively modern and purpose-built, but they occupy prime spots: one on the peak of Madeira's third-highest mountain, the Pico do Arieiro, and the other on the edge of a protected area of virgin forest at the centre of the island.

Shopping Centres and Markets

PLACES TO SHOP

All the shops mentioned in this section are in Funchal, unless otherwise stated.

SHOPPING CENTRES

The late 1990s saw a rash of new shopping malls being built in Funchal. The biggest (with a huge supermarket in the basement) is the Anadia Shopping Centre, located directly opposite the Mercado dos Lavradores (the Workers' Market) on Rua Dr Fernão Omelas. The smartest, with upmarket boutiques and furnishing stores, is the Galerias São Lourenço, opposite the tourist office on Avenida Arriaga.

SHOPPING CENTRES

BAZAR OLIVEIRAS

Everything from honey cake (*bolo de mel*) to videos of Madeira, and from tacky keyrings to sophisticated handmade embroidery is here.

✉ Rua das Murcas 6 ☎ 224 632 🕐 Daily 10–7

CASA DO TURISTA

The Casa do Turista offers a comprehensive selection of Madeiran and Portuguese products. The shop occupies an elegant town house in the centre of Funchal, and lace, embroidery, pottery, glass and furniture are displayed beneath ornate plastered ceilings; fine paintings are displayed on the walls. You can browse for anything from a wicker cache pot to a complete dinner service.

✉ Rua do Conselheiro José Silvestre Ribeiro 2 ☎ 224 907 🕐 Mon–Fri 10–7; Sat 10–1

EDEN MAR SHOPPING CENTRE

In the heart of the Hotel Zone, this shopping centre, which includes a supermarket, clothing shops, banks, art gallery and wine shops, is where most tourists shop.

✉ Rua do Gorgulho ☎ No telephone 🕐 Daily 10–7

MARINA SHOPPING CENTRE

Three floors of shops, from electrical goods and clothing to beachwear and disco gear. Look out for fine leather goods at Sacco et Compa, in the basement, and for men's clothes at Wesley, on street level.

✉ Avenida Arriaga (the end nearest Hotel Zone) 🕐 Mon–Fri 10–7; Sat 10–1 (some shops open all day Sat and Sun)

MARKETS

Although supermarkets exist on Madeira, many people still shop for daily necessities in the local covered market. There is a huge market in Funchal (▶ 33) which operates all day, every day except Sunday. Elsewhere the markets are much smaller and are usually closed by lunchtime – for the best choice you need to arrive before 9:30. Markets are usually divided into two areas, with fish sold from great white marble slabs in one half, and fruits and vegetables artfully displayed in the other half. Delicatessen goods and meat are sold from enclosed shops around the market perimeter.

All the main towns have markets, open from 8 to 1 Monday to Friday:

Ribeira Brava: next to bus station, on seafront road.
Calheta: on seafront road.
Câmara de Lobos: on the road skirting the western side of the harbour.
Santa Cruz: to the west of the Palm Beach lido on the seafront esplanade.
Machico: on the eastern side of the fortress that houses the Tourist Office on the seafront road.
In addition, **Curral das Freiras** hosts a general market in the main street on Sunday mornings.

Books and Home Furnishings

BOOKSHOPS

LIVRARIA PÁTIO

The Pátio Bookshop is housed in several separate shops around the very attractive O Pátio café. Owned by John and Susan Farrow, who also run the English School, the shop has guide books to the island, plus a fascinating range of antiquarian books and best-selling fiction titles in English, French, German and Portuguese. It also stocks a wide range of artists' materials.

✉ Rua da Carreira 43
☎ 224 490 🕐 Mon–Fri 10–7; Sat 10–1

COLLECTABLES

THE COLLECTORS SHOP

Old postcards make an unusual souvenir; browse for postcards, greetings cards, postage stamps, coins, banknotes, medallions and old book covers, as well as minerals and precious stones, at this collectors' cornucopia.

✉ Avenida Arriaga 75
☎ 223 070 🕐 Mon–Fri 10–7; Sat 10–1

FURNISHINGS

CARPETLAND

Oriental rugs.

✉ Rua das Murcas 16–18
☎ 223 522 🕐 Mon–Fri 10–7; Sat 10–1

CAYRES

Modern Portuguese ceramics.

✉ Rua Dr Fernão Ornelas 56A/B ☎ 226 104
🕐 Mon–Fri 10–7; Sat 10–11

HOUSEKEEPER

Fabrics, lighting and decorative products.

✉ Rua dos Arahhas
☎ 228 999 🕐 Mon–Fri 10–7; Sat 10–1

INTEMPORÂNEO INTERIORES

Modern furniture, lighting and furnishing fabrics.

✉ Rua das Netos 18
☎ 238 076 🕐 Mon–Fri 10–1, 3–7; Sat 10–1

O IMAGINÁRIO

Picture frames, ceramics, fabrics and silk flowers, plus a good choice of Portuguese Christmas crib figures and tree decorations.

✉ Rua das Aranhas 34
☎ 230 307 🕐 Mon–Fri 10–7; Sat 10–1

TELA

Boxes made of silver and carved wood, seashells, bird cages – attractive souvenirs.

✉ Rua da Carreira 174
☎ 230 240 🕐 Mon–Fri 10–7; Sat 10–1

TAPESTRY

THE KIEKEBEN SHOP

Finished wall hangings, chair covers, carpets and even luggage and handbags made from tapestry.

✉ Rua da Carreira 194
☎ 222 073 🕐 Mon–Fri 10–7; Sat 10–1

MADEIRA SUN

Do-it-yourself tapestry kits at a fraction of the price you would pay for the finished articles.

✉ Avenida Zarco 4
🕐 Mon–Fri 10–7; Sat 10–1

TAPESTRY

Herbert Kiekeben, a German artist, introduced the craft of sewing pictures on canvas to Madeira in 1938. Though tapestry has not outgrown embroidery in the Madeiran craft league, locally made products now sell worldwide.

Arts and Crafts

MADEIRAN EMBROIDERY

The art of fine embroidery was introduced to Madeira by Elizabeth Phelps, the daughter of an English wine merchant, in the 1850s. This was a time of great calamity on Madeira, with disease having decimated the island's wine crops and cholera raging through the population (7,000 people died in 1852 alone). The resulting poverty so distressed Miss Phelps that she established her embroidery business as a means of supplementing the islanders' meagre incomes. Today 20,000 Madeirans are involved in the business, including men and boys.

KNITWEAR

Knitted cotton sweaters and thick Madeiran hats with ear flaps are sold by roadside stallholders all over Madeira. Though not always in fashionable colours or designs, they are, nevertheless, a bargain.

EMBROIDERY

Madeiran embroidery is made by hand and it takes many hours to produce even a simple napkin – hence the high prices charged for a blouse, nightdress or tablecloth. True Madeiran lace is distinguished from machine-made products (mostly imported from the Far East) by the lead seal attached to each piece after it has been inspected for quality and finish. The seal (which is slowly being replaced by a similarly shaped hologram) is a guarantee of authenticity granted by IBTAM (➤ 52), the island's handicrafts institute. Funchal has many embroidery 'factories' where the designs are pricked out on to fine linen cloth before it is sent to outworkers to be embroidered. Here the finished articles are washed, ironed and inspected before being given their mark of authenticity. It is worth visiting a factory to learn about the process before making your purchase.

CASA REGIONAL

Fine embroidery and Madeiran souvenirs.
✉ Avenida Zarco 15
☎ 224 943 🕐 Mon–Fri 10–7; Sat 10–1

PATRICIO & GOUVEIA

This is one of the best and biggest factories in Madeira, selling garments and table linen.
✉ Rua do Visconde de Anadia 33 ☎ 220 801 🕐 Mon–Fri 10–7; Sat 10–1

LEATHERWORK

Portuguese craftsmanship in leather is renowned. Madeira has a number of shops selling beautifully made goods that cost about half the price they would fetch in Paris, London or Rome.

ARTECOURO

This shop specialises in beautiful leather goods produced by local craftsmen (you can visit the factory where they are made, at Rua Carlos Azevedo Menezes 16).
✉ Rua da Alfândega 15
☎ 237 256 🕐 Mon–Fri 10–7; Sat 10–1

GONÇALVES & SILVA

For a pair of traditional Madeiran leather ankle boots, with turned down tops, visit this workshop in the Zona Velha and watch them being made before you buy.
✉ Rua da Portão de São Tiaga 22 ☎ 934 663 🕐 Mon–Fri 10–7; Sat 10–1

SAFA PELE

A good choice of elegant leather handbags, wallets, briefcases and luggage.
✉ Rua das Murcas 26A
☎ 223 619 🕐 Daily 10–7

WICKERWORK

For the best selection of wickerwork, visit O Relógio in Camacha (➤ 26).

SOUSA & GONÇALVES

Willow furniture and basket-work at factory prices. Large items can be shipped.
✉ Rua do Castanheiro 47
☎ 223 626 🕐 Daily 10–7

Flowers and Wine

FLOWERS

You can buy flowers in the market or from stallholders around Funchal's cathedral square, but if you buy from shops your purchases will be packed in protective boxes so that they will withstand the journey home.

A ROSA

Order your flowers two or three days before your departure and they will be delivered to your hotel on the day you leave.

✉ Rua Imperatriz Dona Amélia 126 ☎ 764 111 🕔 Mon–Fri 10–7; Sat 10–1

BOA VISTA ORCHIDS

Whether you want to buy orchids or not, it is worth visiting Boa Vista Orchids for the lovely subtropical gardens that surround the Quinta da Boa Vista.

✉ Rua Lombo da Boa Vista ☎ 220 468 🕔 Mon–Sat 9–5:30

GARDENIA AZUL

Outside the Savoy Hotel and convenient for the Hotel Zone.

✉ Avenida do Infante ☎ 234 171 🕔 Mon–Fri 10–7; Sat 10–1

JARDIM ORQUÍDEA

The Orchid Garden is a nursery with 4,000 varieties of tropical orchid on display (flowering all year – main season November to February). You can visit the breeding laboratories and buy in vitro plants, grown in gel in a plastic tube to take home. There is an entrance charge.

✉ Rua Pita da Silva 37 ☎ 238 444 🕔 Daily 9–6

MAGNOLIA FLOWER SHOP

Excellent selection of cut and dried flowers, plus pot plants, bulbs and orchids.

✉ Loja 1, Casino Park Hotel Gardens ☎ 222 577 🕔 Daily 10–7

WINE & LIQUEURS

The most enjoyable way to buy wine is to visit a wine lodge, such as Adegas de São Francisco (► 31), where you can sample the products.

ARTUR DE BARROS E SOUSA

Visitors are greeted by the warm evocative smells of old wood and rich wine at this old wine lodge.

✉ Rua dos Ferreiros 109 ☎ 220 622 🕔 Mon–Fri 10–7; Sat 10–1

DIOGOS WINE SHOP

Not only a comprehensive stock of Madeiran and Portuguese wines, but also a Columbus Museum alongside.

✉ Avenida Arriaga 48 ☎ 233 357 🕔 Daily 10–7

D'OLIVEIRAS

A traditional wine lodge with free tastings.

✉ Rua dos Ferreiros 107 ☎ 220 784 🕔 Mon–Fri 10–7; Sat 10–1

HENRIQUES & HENRIQUES

Another long-established wine lodge.

✉ Sítio de Belém, Câmara de Lobos ☎ 941 551 🕔 Mon–Fri 10–7; Sat 10–1

DANCERS ON A STICK

Among Madeiran souvenirs, look out for the percussive musical instruments called *brinquinhos*. These consist of a number of dolls in Madeiran costume, holding cymbals and bells, which clap their hands as you move them up and down a central stick.

Sport

QUINTA DO MAGNÓLIA

The elegant Quinta do Magnólia was built as the British Country Club but now belongs to the Madeiran regional government. Pretty gardens surround the building and, for those in search of exercise, there is a full range of sports facilities, including tennis courts, a large swimming pool, a putting course, squash courts and a jogging track. Entrance is free, and bookings to use the squash and tennis courts should be made at the gatekeeper's lodge at the entrance.

✉ Rua Dr Pita ☎ 764 598
🕐 Daily 7:30AM–9PM

DIVING

ATALAIA DIVING

Operating out of Caniço, Atalaia Diving offers a beginners course leading to the CMAS Bronze qualification, and a programme of dives at sites around the island.

✉ Caniço ☎ 934 330

DIVE COLLEGE INTERNATIONAL

Fully trained and certified instructors offer courses and dives for beginners and experienced divers.

✉ Hotel Dom Pedro Baia, Machico ☎ 965 751

SCORPIO DIVERS

Another long-established diving club offering training courses for beginners, and dives for more experienced divers. Scorpio operates out of the Lido Complex, in Funchal's Hotel Zone, but also offers dives on Porto Santo during the summer.

✉ Complexo do Lido, Funchal ☎ 66977

FISHING

MADEIRA BIG GAME FISHING

Specialists in charter boats for sport fishing, Madeira Fishing offers four- or eight-hour trips for up to eight people.

✉ Funchal Marina ☎ 227 169; www.madeiragamefish.com

TURISPECA

Turispeca specialises in big-game fishing trips. Charters can be for between four and seven hours, and the price includes tackle and bait for up to five anglers. The crews know where to go for the best fishing grounds; depending on the time of year, there are big blue marlin, big-eye tuna, blue-fin tuna, yellow-fin tuna and sharks to catch.

✉ Yachting Marina, Funchal ☎ 231 063

GOLF

MADEIRA GOLF

The 27-hole Madeira Golf Club is set among the wooded hills of Santo da Serra, to whose cool heights wealthy Madeiran merchants used to retreat in the summer. Reservations can be made from most hotels (48 hours notice is recommended) and transport can be arranged from central Funchal. Equipment can be hired and you can attend the regular golf clinics, as well as booking private lessons.

✉ Santo da Serra ☎ 552 345

QUINTA DO PALHEIRO GOLF CLUB

The beautifully wooded and landscaped grounds of the Quinta do Palheiro estate were laid out in the late 18th century by a French gardener working for a wealthy Portuguese aristocrat, the Conde de Carvalhal. Today, part of the estate has been turned into a golf course, renowned for its scenic beauty. The clubhouse, built in the traditional Madeiran style, enjoys fine views over Funchal. The 18-hole course, designed by Cabell Robinson, is a challenging medium-length course of 6,105m, set among 100-year-old pine forest and lush native woodland, with views to the eastern end of the island.

✉ Quinta do Palheiro ☎ 792 116; www.madeira-golf.com

HEALTH CLUBS

Massage, aromatherapy, mud-wraps and facials – not exactly sport but an increasingly popular holiday activity on Madeira. If you feel like being pampered, try the Essentially Natural Health Centre (☎ 706 280 ext. 2067) at Vila Ramos Hotel, or the Thalassothys Spa, at Dorisol Hotel (☎ 702 118).

HORSE RIDING

CLUB IPISMO

Catering for beginners and experienced riders, the Club Ipismo offers the chance to explore hidden parts of Madeira from the back of a horse – more environmentally friendly by far than a jeep safari. Bookings can be made direct, or through Hotel Estrelícia (☎ 706 600).
✉ Caminho dos Pretos, Funchal ☎ 224 982

MOTORSPORTS

MADEIRA WINE RALLY

The ear-ripping sound of high performance engines accelerating through the streets of central Funchal signals the start of the Madeira Wine Rally. The rally takes place during the first week in August. Visitors may find certain roads closed during the rally, especially to the west of the island; the rally route centres around the flat Paúl da Serra plateau between Funchal and Porto do Moniz. You can watch the start and finish of the daily stages in Avenida Arriaga, in central Funchal. All the nearby bars will be full of macho Funchalese, watching the race on television and boasting of their own driving prowess.

SWIMMING

Because Madeira lacks classic sand-sea beaches, the luxury hotels of the hotel district have all invested in high-quality swimming facilities, most of which are open to non-residents for a small fee, which is often waived if you use the hotel's café. Madeira also has some excellent public pools which are under-used outside the main summer season and weekends, so you'll probably enjoy as much privacy as in a private hotel pool. The biggest complex is the Lido, on Rua Gorgulho, in the Hotel Zone (☎ 231 150). Farther out of Funchal is the Clube Naval do Funchal (✉ Estrada Pontinha ☎ 661 224), a civilised spot with pools, sea bathing and a café, kept more exclusive by costing three times as much as the Lido.

TENNIS AND SQUASH

QUINTA DO MAGNÓLIA
► 80, side panel.

BENEATH THE WAVES

Anyone diving off Madeira can expect to see a good range of marine life in the island's clear waters and rocky foreshores. Of the big fish, the majestic manta rays are the most common; these gregarious fish seem to know when divers are about and you can be fairly sure that they will be along to play. Black crabs, the colour of the island's volcanic rocks, are common, as are sea anemones. With luck you may see a coral-coloured scorpion fish or a bright red parrot fish, so-called because of the shape of its beak-like mouth, which is used for prising limpets off the rocks.

Nightlife

MADEIRAN DANCE

Madeira's traditional dance reflects the burdens of rural patterns of work. In the Carrier's Dance, the dancers bend beneath the weight of the imaginary stacks of sugar cane or baskets of bananas they carry along the island's steep paths. In the Heavy Dance, the rhythmic stamping of the dancers' feet reflects the custom of crushing grapes for wine with bare feet.

CABARET

PESTANA CARLTON PARK HOTEL

It would be hard to better this hotel for evening entertainment. As well as dinner dances with live acts in the restaurant, the casino offers three dinner shows. Choose between New York, New York, featuring song and dance routines from Broadway musicals, Brazil Latino, with its hot rhythms and fast-paced dancing, and the Cabaret Festival, an evening of extravagant dance, music and magic.
✉ Rua Imperatriz Dona Amélia, Funchal ☎ 231 121 ◉ All year

CASINOS

CASINO DA MADEIRA

Resembling a volcanic cone – or a rack of lamb, as the locals would have it – the Casino in Funchal is a striking building, designed by Oscar Niemeyer, who created the master plan for the futuristic Brazilian capital, Brasilia. The casino has French and American roulette, Black Jack, French Bank and chemin-de-fer tables, and there are slot machines in the entrance area. In the same complex are the Panoramic restaurant, with its floor show, and the Baccará discotheque. Entrance to the casino is restricted to those aged 18 and over, so passports are required as proof of age.
✉ Avenida do Infante, Funchal ☎ 231 121 ◉ Tue–Sat 9PM–4AM

CINEMA

CINEMAX CINEMA

Funchal's main cinema shows films in their original language with Portuguese subtitles.
✉ Avenida Arriaga, Funchal ☎ 231 933 ◉ Screenings daily at 2, 4:30, 7, 9:30

CLASSICAL MUSIC

Funchal has a thriving musical *conservatoire*, and you may be fortunate enough to catch a concert by students and teachers during your stay. Many of them are organised under the aegis of the Orquestra Clássica da Madeira (☎ 742 793). Ask at the Tourist Office for details or look for posters in town.

DISCOS

O FAROL

Packed during the summer, when top DJs are brought over from mainland Portugal to entertain the holidaying Lisbonites. Quieter and mainly patronised by more affluent oldies during the rest of the year, when top hits of the 1960s are the most popular numbers.
✉ Pestana Carlton Madeira Hotel, Largo António Nobre ☎ 231 031 ◉ Daily 9:30PM–3AM

VESPAS

Vespas has been around for decades and remains everyone's favourite disco on Madeira. It now features a laser show.
✉ Avenida Sa Carneiro, Funchal ☎ 234 800 ◉ Daily midnight–6AM

FOLK DANCING

Just about every hotel on Madeira offers folk-dancing evenings, and you can enjoy the same spectacle if you dine in the seafood restaurants lining the Yachting Marina in Funchal. At the best shows (such as that at the Café Relógio, ► below), the dancers and musicians will explain the origins and history of their dances, instruments and costumes. Folk dancing on Madeira remains rooted in popular culture and there are numerous folklore groups around the island who perform at local festivals.

CAFÉ RELÓGIO

Camacha is the base for one of Madeira's most accomplished folklore groups, and they can be seen in performance nightly at the Café Relógio's Panorama restaurant.
✉ Camacha ☎ 922 777 ⏰ 7–11PM

HOTEL-BASED ENTERTAINMENT

All the major hotels in Funchal's Hotel Zone have entertainment programmes that are also open to non-residents. Noticeboards advertise forthcoming events.

LIVE MUSIC

ARSÉNIO'S

The plaintive style of music known as *fado* (fate) is as popular on Madeira as it is in the back streets of Lisbon, where the style was originally born.

Arsénio's is a good place to go to hear the music performed live as it has a long-established reputation for the quality of the singers and guitarists it brings over to perform from the mainland.
✉ Rua de Santa Maria 169, Funchal ☎ 224 007 ⏰ Daily noon–2AM

MARCELINO FADO HOUSE

If Arsénio's is full or you want to ring the changes, try the newer Marcelino Fado House for bar snacks and wine accompanied by soulful singing and guitar playing.
✉ Travessa da Torre 22A, Funchal ☎ 220 216 ⏰ Daily 8:30PM–4AM

NIGHTCLUBS

O FUGITIVO

Energetic and scantily clad dancers from England and Brazil provide the entertainment at a venue that describes itself as a 'dancing pub'.
✉ Rua Imperatriz Dona Amélia 68, Funchal ☎ 222 003 ⏰ Shows at midnight, 1:30, 3:30AM

THEATRE

Teatro Baltazar Dias, Funchal's gem of a theatre (also known as the Teatro Municipal), is the focal point for the island's cultural life. There is a regular programme of concerts, dance, theatre (usually in Portuguese) and art film. Look out for events advertised outside the theatre, on Avenida Arriaga.

MADEIRAN MUSIC

Musical accompaniment to Madeiran dance is provided by an instrument similar to a ukulele, known as the *braguinha*. Rhythm is provided by wooden castanets, called *castanholes*, and a notched stick, called a *raspadeira*, played like a washboard.

MADEIRA
practical matters

BEFORE YOU GO

WHAT YOU NEED

		UK	Germany	USA	Netherlands	Spain
● Required						
○ Suggested						
▲ Not required						
Passport/National Identity Card		●	●	●	●	●
Visa		▲	▲	▲	▲	▲
Onward or Return Ticket		○	○	○	○	○
Health Inoculations		▲	▲	▲	▲	▲
Health Documentation (➤ 90, Health)		●	●	●	●	●
Travel Insurance		○	○	○	○	○
Driving Licence (national with Portuguese translation or international)		●	●	●	●	●
Car Insurance Certificate (if own car)		●	●	●	●	●
Car Registration Document (if own car)		●	●	●	●	●

WHEN TO GO

Funchal

High season

Low season

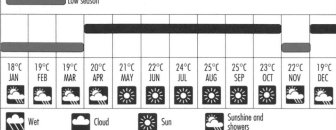

18°C JAN	19°C FEB	19°C MAR	20°C APR	21°C MAY	22°C JUN	24°C JUL	25°C AUG	25°C SEP	23°C OCT	22°C NOV	19°C DEC

☔ Wet   ☁ Cloud   ☀ Sun   🌦 Sunshine and showers

TIME DIFFERENCES

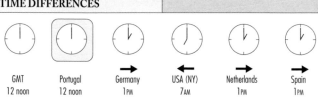

GMT	Portugal	Germany	USA (NY)	Netherlands	Spain
12 noon	12 noon	1PM	7AM	1PM	1PM

TOURIST OFFICES

In the UK
Portuguese National Tourist Office
22–25A Sackville Street
London W1X 1DE
☎ 0207 494 5725
Fax: 0207 494 1868

In the USA
Portuguese National Tourist Office
590 Fifth Avenue, 4th Floor
New York, NY 10036
☎ 212/354 4403
Fax: 212/764 6137

WHEN YOU ARE THERE

ARRIVING

Cruise ships regularly call at Funchal on the way to the Caribbean, but most visitors to Madeira arrive by air. Santa Catarina airport is served by flights from most European airports, either direct or via Lisbon. TAP Air Portugal is the national airline (in Funchal ☎ 239 210; fax: 239 248).

Santa Catarina Airport to Funchal	Journey times	
22 kilometres		N/A
	🚌	50 minutes
	🚕	35 minutes

MONEY

The euro is the official currency of Portugal.
Euro banknotes and coins were introduced in January 2002. Banknotes are in denominations of 5, 10, 20, 50, 100, 200 and 500 euros; coins are in denominations of 1, 2, 5, 10, 20 and 50 cents, and 1 and 2 euros. Major credit cards are widely accepted. Credit and debit cards can also be used for withdrawing euro notes from ATM machines.

TIME

 Madeira, like mainland Portugal, observes Greenwich Mean Time during the winter months; during the summer, from late March to late September, the time is GMT plus one hour.

CUSTOMS

YES

From an EU country for personal use (guidelines):
800 cigarettes, 200 cigars, 1 kilogram of tobacco
10 litres of spirits (over 22%)
20 litres of aperitifs
90 litres of wine, of which 60 litres can be sparkling wine
110 litres of beer

From a non-EU country for personal use:
200 cigarettes OR 50 cigars OR 250 grams of tobacco
1 litre of spirits (over 22%)
2 litres of intermediary products (eg sherry) and sparkling wine
2 litres of still wine
50 grams of perfume
0.25 litres of eau de toilette
The value limit for goods is €175.

Travellers under 17 years of age are not entitled to the tobacco and alcohol allowances.

When returning home, note that some countries place restrictions on the import of plant material.

NO

Narcotic drugs, firearms, ammunition, offensive weapons, obscene material, unlicensed animals.

CONSULATES

UK ☎ 221 221	Germany ☎ 220 338	USA ☎ 743 429	Netherlands ☎ 223 890

TOURIST OFFICES

Funchal
● Avenida Arriaga 16
☎ 225 658
Fax: 232 151
email: info@madeira-tourism.org

Machico
● Forte de Nossa Senhora do Amparo
☎ 962 289

Porto Santo
● Rua Dr Vieira da Castro
☎ 982 361

Ribeira Brava
● Forte de São Bento
☎ 951 675

Santana
● Sítio do Serrado
☎ 572 992

Some travel agencies in Funchal advertise themselves as if they were tourist information centres, though their primary aim is to sell you one of their organised tours. In general these tours (by minibus or coach) are good value and the standards of safety are high. You must expect, however, that the tour will include time spent in shops and restaurants rather than sightseeing — you may prefer to have the flexibility of your own taxi with driver, which can be as cheap as an organised tour if three or four people share a car.

NATIONAL HOLIDAYS

J	F	M	A	M	J	J	A	S	O	N	D
1	2	(2)	(3)	1	2	1	2		1	1	4

1 Jan	New Year's Day
Feb (dates vary)	Shrove Tuesday, Ash Wednesday
Mar/Apr	Good Friday, Easter Monday
25 Apr	Day of the Revolution
1 May	Labour Day
Jun (dates vary)	Corpus Christi
10 Jun	National Day
1 Jul	Madeira Day
15 Aug	Feast of the Assumption
21 Aug	Funchal Day
5 Oct	Republic Day
1 Nov	All Saints' Day
1 Dec	Restoration of Independence Day
8 Dec	Immaculate Conception
25/26 Dec	Christmas

OPENING HOURS

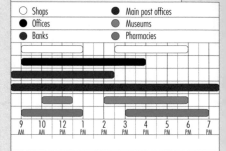

○ Shops	● Main post offices
● Offices	● Museums
● Banks	● Pharmacies

9 AM 10 AM 12 PM 1 PM 2 PM 3 PM 4 PM 5 PM 6 PM 7 PM

Small shops and those catering to tourists are open daily from around 8AM until 7 or 8PM, including Sundays and public holidays. Larger stores and supermarkets increasingly ignore the lunch break and are open continuously from 9–7. Some supermarkets stay open until 10 (5 on Sunday). Pharmacies open late on a duty rota (posted on pharmacy doors). Village post offices have shorter opening hours; main post offices also open on Saturday mornings.

ELECTRICITY

The power supply on Madeira is: 220 volts AC.

Sockets accept Continental two-pronged plugs, so an adaptor is needed for non-Continental appliances, and a transformer for appliances operating on 100–120 volts.

TIPS/GRATUITIES

Yes ✓ No ✗		
Tipping is appreciated but not required on Madeira		
Restaurants (service and tax included)	✓	10%
Bar service	✓	change
Taxis	✓	10%
Tour guides	✓	€1.50
Chambermaids	✗	No
Swimming pool attendants	✓	change
Porters	✓	€1.50
Hairdressers	✓	10%
Toilets	✗	No

PUBLIC TRANSPORT

Internal Flights
There are several flights a day from Funchal to Porto Santo. The 37km journey takes 15 minutes, and flights are heavily booked in high season, so be sure to book well in advance. Flights can be booked through any travel agent or through branches of TAP Air Portugal. On Madeira, TAP's office is at Avenida das Comunidades Madeirenses 10 (☎ 239 210).

Buses
A highly efficient bus system connects all towns with Funchal. Buses are modern and comfortable (although they do not have safety belts and some journeys can be hair-raising on Madeira's tortuous roads). Buses within Funchal and its suburbs are painted orange; those serving the rural areas are operated by five different companies, each with its own livery. Nearly all buses depart from the bus stops along Avenida do Mar, where you can also buy tickets from the bus company kiosks (7-day go-as-you-please passes are available to visitors only, so bring your passport if you want to buy one). Up-to-date timetables are available from the Tourist Office on Avenida Arriaga 16.

Boat Trips
The *Lobo Marinho* ferry serving Porto Santo departs from the pier (*pontinha*) next to the yachting marina in Funchal daily (except Tuesday). Tickets can be bought in advance from travel agents, or from the pier just before sailing. Further information from the Porto Santo Line, Rua da Praia 4, Funchal ☎ 210 300). A number of cruise companies operate out of Funchal's yachting marina, all offering half- or full-day excursions around Madeira's coastline. Turispeca (☎ 231 063) operates charter cruises, game-fishing trips and regular cruises (including evening cruises with dinner).

CAR HIRE

The major car hire firms are represented on Madeira, as well as several local companies, which offer competitive rates. You can book a car in advance through travel agents, at the airport on arrival or through your hotel. All rental firms will deliver your car to you.

TAXIS

There are taxi ranks in towns and taxis may also stop if flagged down, especially in the countryside. Rates for out-of-town journeys (eg from Funchal to the airport) are fixed. Short journeys are metered. For longer journeys, you can negotiate an hourly or half-day rate.

CONCESSIONS

Students/youths Museums have lower rates of admission for students, and entry is free for children. Bring a passport or student card as proof of your age.

Senior Citizens Many senior citizens come to Madeira for the winter months, attracted by warm weather, a low cost of living and heavily discounted low-season long-stay rates. Ask travel agents specialising in Madeira for details.

DRIVING

Speed limit on motorways: **100kph**

Speed limit on main roads: **80kph**

Speed limit on urban roads: **60 or 40 kph**

It is mandatory for drivers and passengers to wear seat belts if fitted.

Breath testing: random tests are carried out.

Petrol (*gasolina*) comes in two grades: lead-free (*sem chumbo*) and lead-substitute (*super*). Diesel (*gasóleo*) is also available. Most villages and towns have a petrol station, and they are generally open from 8 to 8. The GALP petrol station on Avenida do Infante, in Funchal, is open 24 hours. Most take credit cards.

Because all visitors to Madeira drive rental cars, there is no central breakdown and rescue service. Instead, the car rental companies operate their own breakdown services, with repairs usually being carried out promptly. The documents you are given on hiring the car will explain what to do in the event of a breakdown.

PHOTOGRAPHY

What to photograph: Madeira's mountainous landscape will provide you with many subjects, including waterfalls, sheer cliffs, volcanic landscapes and deep ravines. For colour, there are markets, flowers and traditional costumes.
Best time to photograph: the light is best before 10AM, after which time you can expect haze and clouds. Madeira's sunsets are brief but colourful.
Film and camera batteries are available from most hotels, and there are specialist photo shops, also offering processing services, in central Funchal.

PERSONAL SAFETY

Crime on Madeira is extremely rare. In the unlikely event that you are the victim of theft, report your loss to the main police station at the Rua Dr João de Deus 7 (☎ 222 022) and get a copy of the written statement to support your insurance claim.

To help prevent crime:
- Leave your valuables in the hotel.
- Do not leave unattended valuables on the beach or poolside.
- Beware of pickpockets in markets and on crowded streets.

Police, fire, ambulance:
☎ **112**
from any call box

TELEPHONES

Telephones are found in cafés and on the streets of larger towns. Some only take phonecards, available from newsagents and cafés. To call Madeira or Porto Santo from the UK, dial 00 351 (the international code for Portugal), then 291 (the area code for both islands). In Madeira and Porto Santo you need dial only the subscriber number.

International Dialling Codes From Madeira (Portugal) to:	
UK:	00 44
Germany:	00 49
Netherlands:	00 31
Spain:	00 34
USA:	00 1

POST

Post Offices
Post offices (correios) are found in the main towns. In Funchal, the most central post office is on Avenida do Zarco. Poste Restante services are available at the main post office on Rua Dr João Brito Camara. Stamps can also be bought from many newsagents. Open: Mon–Fri 8:30–8; Sat 9–12:30.

HEALTH

Insurance
Nationals of EU countries receive free emergency medical treatment on Madeira with the relevant documentation (form E111 for Britons), although private medical insurance is still advised and is essential for all other visitors.

Dental Services
Dental services on Madeira are excellent. Dentists advertise their services in the free English- and German-language magazines that are available from most hotels and the tourist information centre in Funchal.

Sun Advice
The sun can be intense on Madeira at any time of the year, and it is possible to burn with less than an hour's exposure. If you are out walking on bare mountains, it is best to cover vulnerable parts of your body, including your neck, legs and arms.

Drugs
Chemists (farmácia) are open Mon–Fri 9–1 and 3–7, and Sat 9–12:30. Some open through the lunch break, and there is a late-night duty rota, posted in pharmacy windows. Take supplies of any drugs that you take regularly, since there is no guarantee that they will be available locally.

Safe Water
Tap water is safe to drink everywhere. The water is fresh and often comes straight from pure mountain springs. Mineral water is available everywhere; if you ask for fizzy water (água com gás), rather than still (água sem gás), it is likely to be naturally sparkling, rather than carbonated.

WHEN YOU ARE THERE

LANGUAGE

Portuguese is the language of Madeira, but most hoteliers, shopkeepers and restaurateurs speak English and German as well. Portuguese is easy to understand in its written form if you already know a Romance language – such as Latin, French, Italian or Spanish. When pronounced, however, it could easily be mistaken for a Slavic language. Two sounds are distinctive to Portuguese: vowels accented with a tilda sound like *owoo* (so bread, *pão*, is pronounced *powoo*) and the s and z, which are pronounced *zsh* (so *carros*, cars, is pronounced *carrozsh*).

hotel	hotel/estalagem	twin room	quarto com duas camas
do you have a room?	tem um quarto livre?	with bathroom	com banho
I have a reservation	tenho um quarto reservado	one night	um noite
how much per night?	qual e o preço por noite?	key	chave
a single room	um quarto simples	sea view	vista a mar
double room	quarto de casal	gents/ladies	senhores/senhoras

bank	um banco	pounds/dollars	libras/dólares
exchange office	câmbios	do you take?	aceitam?
post office	correio	credit card	cartão de crédito
coins	moedas		
banknotes	notas	traveller's cheque	cheque de viagem
receipt	recibo	cheque	cheque
the change	troco	how much?	quanta custa?
can you change?	pode trocar?		

breakfast	pequeno almoço	beer	cerveja
lunch	almoço	menu	lista
dinner	jantar	red wine	vinho tinto
table	mesa	white wine	vinho branco
starter	entrada	water	água
main course	prato principal	tea	chá
dessert	sobremesa	coffee (black)	um bica
bill	conta	coffee (white)	café con leite

airport	aeroporto	how far?	a que distância?
bus	autocarro	where is?	onde está?
bus station	estação de autocarros	car	carro
bus stop	paragem	petrol	gasolina
a ticket to	um bilhete para	petrol station	posto de gasolina
single	ida		
return	ide e volta		
which way to?	como se vai para?		

yes	sim	you're welcome	está bem
no	não	how are you?	camo está?
please	faz favor	well, thank you	bem, obrigado (a)
thank you (male)	obrigado	not at all	de nada
thank you (female)	obrigada	do you speak English?	fala inglês?
hello	olá	I don't understand	não compreendo
goodbye	adeus		
good morning	bom dia		
good afternoon	boa tarde		
good evening/night	boa noite		
excuse me	desculpe		

WHEN DEPARTING

REMEMBER

- Funchal airport is small and does not have extensive shopping facilities.
- High winds can occasionally disrupt flights into and out of Madeira, in which case incoming flights are diverted to Porto Santo, and outgoing flights are delayed. Late October/early November are the riskiest periods.
- Arrive at the airport no later than the check-in time stated on your ticket.

Index

TwinPack
Madeira

Written by   Christopher Catling
Edited, designed and produced by AA Publishing
Maps   © Automobile Association Developments Limited 2002
Fold-out map   © Freytag-Berndt u. Artaria KG, 1231 Vienna-Austria, all rights reserved

Published and distributed by AA Publishing, a trading name of Automobile Association
Developments Limited, whose registered office is Millstream, Maidenhead Road, Windsor,
Berkshire, SL4 5GD. Registered number 1878835

The contents of this book are believed correct at the time of printing. Nevertheless, the publishers
cannot be held responsible for any errors or omissions or for changes in the details given in this
guide or for the consequences of any reliance on the information it provides. Assessments of
attractions, hotels, restaurants and other sights are based upon the author's personal experience
and, therefore, necessarily contain elements of subjective opinion which may not reflect the
publishers' opinion or dictate a reader's own experiences on another occasion.

We have tried to ensure accuracy in this guide, but things do change and we would be grateful if
readers would advise us of any inaccuracies they may encounter.

A CIP catalogue record for this book is available from the British Library.

ISBN 0 7495 3458 3

Colour separation by Chroma Graphics Overseas (PTE) Ltd, Singapore
Printed in Malaysia

ACKNOWLEDGEMENTS
The Automobile Association wishes to thank the following for their assistance in the preparation
of this book:
DIRECÇÃO REGIONAL DE TOURISMO, MADEIRA 48b; PORTO SANTO DIVING CENTRE 43b.
The remaining pictures used in this publication are held in the Automobile Association's own
photo library (AA Photo Library) and were taken by the following photographers:
PETER BAKER F/Cover (a) Santana, (b) Garajau, B/Cover Monte, 12t, 14t, 18, 21t, 21b, 23b, 26t,
27b, 30t, 30b, 31t, 33t, 38, 40t, 40b, 45t, 45b, 49t, 50, 51, 55, 56, 61t, 85b, 90t, 90bl; TONY
OLIVER 20; CLIVE SAWYER F/Cover (c) girl in costume, (d) Santa Clara Convent, (e) Flower
festival, (g) flowers, bottom Funchal Square, 5t, 5b, 7, 24t, 25, 27t, 28t, 29t, 29b, 36b, 39t, 41t,
41b, 44t, 46t, 48t; JON WYAND F/Cover (f) chimney detail, 1, 6t, 6b, 8, 12b, 13t, 13b, 14b, 15, 16,
17t, 17b, 19, 23t, 24b, 26b, 28b, 31b, 32t, 32b, 33b, 34t, 34b, 35t, 35b, 36t, 37t, 37b, 39b, 42, 43t,
44b, 46b, 47t, 47b, 49b, 52, 53t, 53b, 54, 57, 58, 59, 60, 61b, 84, 85t, 90br.

TITLES IN THE TWINPACK SERIES
• Cyprus • Gran Canaria • Lanzarote & Fuerteventura • Madeira • Mallorca • Malta & Gozo •
• Menorca • Tenerife •

Dear **TwinPack** Traveller

Your comments, opinions and recommendations are very important to us. So please help us to improve our travel guides by taking a few minutes to complete this simple questionnaire.

You do not need a stamp (unless posted outside the UK). If you do not want to cut this page from your guide, then photocopy it or write your answers on a plain sheet of paper.

Send to: **The Editor, AA TwinPack Travel Guides, FREEPOST SCE 4598, Basingstoke RG21 4GY.**

Your recommendations...

We always encourage readers' recommendations for restaurants, nightlife or shopping – if your recommendation is used in the next edition of the guide, we will send you a *FREE* **AA TwinPack Guide** of your choice. Please state below the establishment name, location and your reasons for recommending it.

_____

_____

_____

_____

Please send me **AA TwinPack**

Cyprus ❑ Gran Canaria ❑ Lanzarote & Fuerteventura ❑ Madeira ❑
Mallorca ❑ Malta & Gozo ❑ Menorca ❑ Tenerife ❑
(*please tick as appropriate*)

About this guide...

Which title did you buy?
AA *TwinPack* _____

Where did you buy it? _____

When? m m / y y

Why did you choose an AA *TwinPack* Guide? _____

_____

_____

_____

_____

Did this guide meet your expectations?
Exceeded ❑ Met all ❑ Met most ❑ Fell below ❑
Please give your reasons _____

_____

_____

continued on next page...

Were there any aspects of this guide that you particularly liked? _____

_____

_____

_____

Is there anything we could have done better? _____

_____

_____

_____

_____

About you...

Name (*Mr/Mrs/Ms*) _____

Address _____

_____

_____ Postcode _____

Daytime tel no _____

Which age group are you in?

Under 25 ☐   25–34 ☐   35–44 ☐   45–54 ☐   55–64 ☐   65+ ☐

How many trips do you make a year?

Less than one ☐   One ☐   Two ☐   Three or more ☐

Are you an AA member? Yes ☐   No ☐

About your trip...

When did you book? m m / y y   When did you travel? m m / y y

How long did you stay? _____

Was it for business or leisure? _____

Did you buy any other travel guides for your trip?

If yes, which ones? _____

_____

Thank you for taking the time to complete this questionnaire. Please send it to us as soon as

possible, and remember, you do not need a stamp (*unless posted outside the UK*).

Happy Holidays!